Your First Step to
Celebrate Recovery ®

INTRODUCTION BY RICK WARREN

Your First Step to
Celebrate
Recovery®

JOHN BAKER

AUTHOR'S NOTE:

Because I have picked up a variety of quotes and slogans from numerous recovery meetings, tapes, and seminars, I have not been able to provide some sources for all of the material here. If you feel that I have quoted your material, please let me know and I will be pleased to give you the credit.

ZONDERVAN REFLECTIVE

Your First Step to Celebrate Recovery
Copyright © 2012 by John Baker

Requests for information should be addressed to:
Zondervan, 3900 Sparks Dr., Grand Rapids, Michigan 49546

ISBN 978-0-310-12544-0 (softcover)

ISBN 978-0-310-13034-5 (audio)

ISBN 978-0-310-69478-6 (ebook)

Published in association with the literary agency RKW Legacy Partners LP, 29881 Santa Margarita Parkway, Rancho Santa Margarita, CA 92688.

Cover design: Brand Navigation
Cover photography: David Robbins / Getty Images
Interior design: Michelle Espinosa

Printed in the United States of America

22 23 24 25 26 27 28 29 30 31 /BVGM/ 15 14 13 12 11 10 9 8 7 6 5

CONTENTS

Introduction

WHAT IS CELEBRATE RECOVERY?

BY RICK WARREN

The Bible clearly states "all have sinned." It is my nature to sin, and it is yours too. None of us is untainted. Because of sin, we've all hurt ourselves, we've all hurt other people, and others have hurt us. This means each of us needs recovery in order to live our lives the way God intended.

You've undoubtedly heard the expression "time heals all wounds." Unfortunately, it isn't true. As a pastor, I frequently talk with people who are still carrying hurts from thirty or forty years ago. The truth is, time often makes things worse. Wounds that are left untended fester and spread infection throughout your entire body. Time only extends the pain if the problem isn't dealt with.

Celebrate Recovery® is a biblical and balanced program that helps us overcome our hurts, hang-ups, and habits. It is based on the actual words of Jesus rather than psychological theory. Celebrate Recovery is more effective in helping us change than anything else I've seen or heard of. Over the years I've seen how God has used this program to transform literally thousands of lives at Saddleback Church and to help people grow toward full Christlike maturity.

Most people are familiar with the classic 12-Step program of AA and other groups. While undoubtedly many lives have been helped through the 12 Steps, I've always been uncomfortable with that program's vagueness about the nature of God, the saving power of Jesus Christ, and the ministry of the Holy Spirit. So I began an intense study of the Scriptures to discover what God had to say about "recovery." To my amazement, I found the principles of recovery—in their logical order—given by Christ in His most famous message, the Sermon on the Mount.

My study resulted in a ten-week series of messages called "The Road to Recovery." During that series, Pastor John Baker developed the participant's guides which became the heart of our Celebrate Recovery program. I believe that this program is unlike any recovery program you may have seen. There are six features that make it unique.

1. *Celebrate Recovery is based on God's Word, the Bible.* When Jesus taught the Sermon on the Mount, He began by stating eight ways to be happy. Today we call them the Beatitudes. From a conventional viewpoint, most of these statements don't make sense. They sound like contradictions. But when you fully understand what Jesus is saying, you'll realize that these eight principles are God's road to recovery, wholeness, growth, and spiritual maturity.

2. *Celebrate Recovery is forward-looking.* Rather than wallowing in the past or dredging up and rehearsing painful memories over and over, we confront our past and move on. Celebrate Recovery focuses on the future. Regardless of what has already happened, the solution is to start making wise choices now and depend on Christ's power to help us make those changes.

3. *Celebrate Recovery emphasizes personal responsibility.* Instead of playing the "accuse and excuse" game of victimization, this program helps us face up to our own poor choices and deal with what we can do something about. We cannot control all that happens to us, but we can control how we respond to everything. That is a secret of happiness. When we stop wasting time fixing the blame, we have more energy to fix the problem. When we stop hiding our own faults and stop hurling accusations at others,

then the healing power of Christ can begin working in our mind, will, and emotions.

4. *Celebrate Recovery emphasizes spiritual commitment to Jesus Christ.* The third principle calls for us to make a total surrender of our lives to Christ. Lasting recovery cannot happen without this principle. Everybody needs Jesus.

5. *Celebrate Recovery utilizes the biblical truth that we need each other in order to grow spiritually and emotionally.* It is built around small group interaction and the fellowship of a caring community. There are many therapies, growth programs, and counselors today that operate around one-to-one interaction. But Celebrate Recovery is built on the New Testament principle that we don't get well by ourselves. We need each other. Fellowship and accountability are two important components of spiritual growth.

6. *Celebrate Recovery addresses all types of hurts, hang-ups, and habits.* Some recovery programs deal only with alcohol or drugs or another single problem. But Celebrate Recovery is a "large umbrella" program under which a limitless number of issues can be dealt with. At Saddleback Church, only one out of three who attend Celebrate Recovery is dealing with alcohol or drugs. We have many other specialized groups.

I'm excited that you have decided to begin the Celebrate Recovery journey. You are going to see your life change in dramatic ways. You are going to experience freedom from your life's hurts, hang-ups, and habits as you allow Jesus to be Lord in every area of your life. To God be the glory! I'll be praying for you.

Chapter 1

WHY DID CELEBRATE RECOVERY GET STARTED?

You are not alone.

In the small city of West Monroe, Louisiana, men and women meet at Celebrate Recovery to share the hurts, hang-ups, and habits that have affected their lives. In greater Atlanta, Georgia, sixty-five churches are safe places where people come to Celebrate Recovery to find victory over their past. Elementary, junior high, and senior high school students are meeting in their own groups to talk about their hurts. In jails and prisons across the country, men and women are meeting in small groups to work through the participant's guides and the eight recovery principles based on the Beatitudes found in Matthew, chapter 5. Regularly, men and women from churches across the United States are making trips to countries such as Rwanda, Brazil, Great Britain, and Australia, to name a few, to share Jesus Christ as the one and only true Higher Power who can help them on their road to recovery.

You are not alone.

This book will help you understand how Celebrate Recovery got started, what the program is based on, and what to expect the first time you come to a Celebrate Recovery meeting. In addition, we will answer the questions that you may have as you begin this exciting, life-changing adventure.

I have asked my wife, Cheryl, to share with you our journey through recovery and how God's vision of Celebrate Recovery was born.

Cheryl and John's Story

I was born in St. Louis, Missouri. My dad was an Air Force sergeant and my mother loyally followed him throughout the United States as well as overseas. Alcohol was prevalent in my home, but my parents assured me that it was not a problem because they didn't drink at work, they just enjoyed the taste of beer, and they could quit whenever they wanted. I noticed that my parents were different after they drank, and I observed that my friends' parents drank very little, but I wanted very much to believe Mom and Dad's behavior was normal.

My mom had polio as a child and suffered a great deal of pain. She spent a lot of time in hospitals after surgeries and felt abandoned and alone. She said she could not believe in a God who would allow little children to feel such agony. Our family never went to church. When friends invited my brother and me, we were discouraged to attend.

By the time I was sixteen, we had lived in Missouri, Texas, Kentucky, New York, Portugal, Japan, and England. I learned early on how to use masks to hide my feelings of insecurity, to accept everyone, and to use a sense of humor when things got uncomfortable. These skills helped me to make friends by the end of the first day of every new school transfer.

My dad retired from the Air Force in the city where I was born, St. Louis, where I began to attend college. At a fraternity-sorority football game, I met John. At the party after the game, John told me that because he was president of his fraternity and I was president of my sorority, it was our "duty" to start off the dancing. Months later, I learned that John had arranged that entire evening so that he could meet me. (Years later, in Celebrate Recovery, I learned this was very manipulative and controlling!)

As John and I began dating, I learned that his childhood was very different from mine. He had been raised as an only child and had lived in a small town, Collinsville, Illinois, his entire life. Two years before John was born, his parents had given birth to a baby boy who died during his first few days of life. His mother never quite got over the pain of the baby's death, but her small Baptist church helped her deal with the loss. John grew up in that church and accepted Jesus into his heart at age thirteen.

It appeared that John had many successes while in high school: he was class president and lettered in baseball, basketball, and track. But John never felt that he was quite good enough. He was always certain that he was letting someone down—his parents, teammates, friends, and girlfriends. While searching for a college to attend, John had applied to several Christian universities to pursue a position in ministry. However, his feelings of low self-esteem caused him to feel unworthy to answer God's call, so he decided on the state university instead.

As soon as John arrived at college, he joined a fraternity and found the solution to all of his problems—alcohol. While he was the life of the party—it didn't start until he got there and wasn't over until he left—I approached the sorority life with caution. I had seen the effects of alcohol at home, and I was afraid that I might be someone who would not be able to handle it well. I didn't drink at all until I was twenty-one, and then I drank very little.

I was aware that John drank a lot in college, but I wanted to believe that it was normal behavior for someone just enjoying the college experience. I did not want to see it as a problem. Despite the warning signs, we got married in our senior year of school. We did not want to wait because we anticipated that John would be called to serve in the war in Vietnam.

John attended Officer Training School and pilot training, and he learned to act like an officer and drink like a gentleman. Again, it continued to cover his pain of low self-worth. He even discovered that the 100 percent oxygen in the plane could cure morning hangovers! When the war ended, he was assigned to a reserve unit and quickly began to pursue a business career. He joined a paper company and earned his masters' degree in business in night school.

After being married for four years, John and I had our first child, our daughter, Laura, and two years later, our son, Johnny, was born. John had been persistent in talking to me about accepting Christ. After our daughter was born, I did accept Him as my Lord and Savior. However, our church attendance was very irregular.

A few years later, when our son started attending a Christian preschool, Johnny explained to me that we could go back to his school on Sundays to hear more stories about Jesus. This tugged at my heart, and we finally committed to our first church home. Meanwhile, John continued to be promoted at work. He was achieving all of his life's goals before the age of thirty.

Each time John was promoted, our family moved. I was following in my parents' footsteps and going from city to city. I worried that my children would have feelings of insecurity from so many relocations. I also noticed that with each business success, John seemed unhappier. He certainly wasn't the life of the party anymore. He drank more and more and got quieter and quieter. I didn't know what to do or whom to turn to. I didn't want my children raised in an alcoholic home. By this time, church had become very important to me. I even taught preschool at our church, but I didn't feel like I could tell anyone there about our struggles. Everyone at church looked and acted as if their lives were perfect. The kids and I already felt different enough because John wasn't attending church with us anymore.

Gradually, things began to change between John and me. We didn't seem to understand one another, and we talked less and less. At first, I thought our relationship was shifting because of all of our relocations—we had moved seven times in the first eleven years of marriage. Or maybe we were losing touch because he traveled so much with his job. But I could see that his drinking was increasing and his relationship with our family was changing. He was emotionally distant and uninterested in our lives.

Each time I confronted John about his drinking, he assured me that it was not a problem, because he did not drink at work, he just enjoyed the taste of beer, and he could quit whenever he wanted. But even though I had grown up with those words, they had a different impact on me as a wife and mother. If he could "just quit whenever he wanted," then why didn't he quit? Maybe there was something about me that caused John to keep drinking. Maybe if I were prettier, or smarter, or funnier, or if I just worked harder, maybe then John would quit drinking. Since we didn't tell anyone about these struggles, to the outside world we looked like an average, normal family.

John began to be defensive about his drinking. He had grown up in the church and was starting to feel uncomfortable with some of his choices: his relationships with our family, his work practices, and the steady increase in the amount of alcohol. He knew that he had a choice—to continue to live by the world's standards or to repent and turn to God. Proverbs 14:12 (TLB) says, "Before every man there lies a wide and pleasant road that seems right but ends in death." But John turned his back on God, and the drinking escalated.

Our family continued to live as if the drinking was not affecting us. After all, John told me repeatedly, he had never lost a job due to alcohol. He had never even gotten pulled over by the police for drunk driving. He wanted so much to convince us that he was a normal, social drinker.

However, when John began drinking beer for breakfast, I knew that we had to face the family secret. John was an alcoholic. This time when I confronted him in anger, I gave him an ultimatum: quit drinking or leave our home. I was completely surprised when he packed his suitcase and announced that we were separating after twenty years of marriage.

Finally, the attempt to cover up John's hurts, hang-ups, and habits with alcohol was causing the breakup of our family. At first, alcohol seemed to be the solution to help him with his low self-esteem, but now it had become the problem in his life that was affecting him emotionally, mentally, physically, and most importantly, spiritually.

While on a business trip in Salt Lake City, John came to the realization that he could not take another drink, but he had no idea how he was going to live without one. Although he did not realize it, he had come to the first Christ-centered recovery step: *We admitted we were powerless over our addictions and compulsive behaviors, that our lives had become unmanageable.* "For I know that good itself does not dwell in me, that is, in my sinful nature. For I have the desire to do what is good, but I cannot carry it out" (Romans 7:18).

He had finally hit his bottom. He went back home and attended his first Alcoholics Anonymous meeting and attended over ninety meetings in ninety days. Then he became ready for Step 2: *We came to believe that a power greater than ourselves could restore us to sanity.* "For it is God who works in you to will and to act in order to fulfill his good purpose" (Philippians 2:13).

As it became clear to John that God loved him unconditionally, he began to find hope. It was time to make the decision to turn over his life and will to the care of God. This was a departure from the secular program he was attending where a "higher power" was very vague. As a child, he had learned who his Higher Power was: Jesus Christ!

John's stubborn willpower had left him empty and broken. The definition of willpower had to change. Willpower now became the willingness to accept God's power for his life. He began to accept, "I can't, God can, and I decide to let Him, one day at a time." He was ready for the third step: *We made a decision to turn our lives and our wills over to the care of God.* "Therefore, I urge you, brothers, in view of God's mercy, to offer your bodies as living sacrifices, holy and pleasing to God — this is your spiritual act of worship" (Romans 12:1).

God provided a sponsor to help navigate the road to recovery. The sponsor taught John that recovery is not meant to be a journey that is traveled alone — we need others to help us. He helped

John stay balanced and didn't judge him. He guided him through the fourth step: *We made a searching and fearless moral inventory of ourselves.* "Let us examine our ways and test them, and let us return to the LORD" (Lamentations 3:40).

Finally, John had to take a look at that young boy from Illinois and face the hurts, hang-ups, and habits that he had attempted to drown with alcohol for all those years. He discovered how the loss of his brother as an infant had impacted his family and affected his low self-esteem. This inventory made it clear that his alcoholism had destroyed all of his important relationships.

In Step 5 he learned: *We admitted to God, to ourselves, and to another human being the exact nature of our wrongs.* "Therefore confess your sins to each other and pray for each other so that you may be healed" (James 5:16). Finally, John was able to face the truth of his past and to accept the forgiveness of Jesus, which led him "out of darkness into his wonderful light."

I was completely unaware that John was beginning to deal with his alcoholism. I was busy putting all of my energies into using a mask, once again, to hide my pain. It was important to look as though nothing was wrong—I had to "hold it together." This is when my dysfunctions really began to surface. I had never told anyone about the breakup of our marriage. I didn't even tell my parents until they came to visit us seven months into the separation. I wanted so much to tell my close Christian friends at the church preschool where I worked, but I just didn't feel safe. I was afraid they might judge me. I didn't think they would understand. As I looked around my church, I wondered if there were others who were also struggling with pain that they were too afraid to share and feeling so different and alone.

Thinking that if we switched churches we would find a safe place to tell others about our pain, the kids and I began attending Saddleback Church. But we didn't want to feel different or alone, so we didn't tell anyone there about the separation either.

I was afraid that the church where I worked would judge me if they learned about the separation, so I accepted the position as the director of another preschool. This job paid more—and the pastor was understanding of my situation. The preschool had 400 families, 50 women on staff, and as I learned my first day on the job, was $40,000 in debt. The first thing I was expected to accomplish was for the school to pay back the money.

Up until this point, I had done a good job of pretending that I could manage all of the changes in my life. But after the first day of my new job, I fell apart. I couldn't stop crying as the pain of the drinking, the failed marriage, and now the impossible job came together. I couldn't believe it when John arrived at the house to visit the kids and to find out how my first day on the job had gone. I was embarrassed to have lost control, but I didn't seem to be able to do anything about it.

As I was crying about the job, I noticed that John had tears in his eyes as he tried to comfort me. He asked what he could do to help and offered suggestions. I realized that we were having a loving conversation—he seemed to be hurting right alongside me. This was confusing to me. John was showing signs of changing, and I had no idea how to cope.

Although I didn't know it at the time, I began working Steps 1 through 3. I knew I was completely powerless to get through the separation by myself. I began to trust Jesus and to lean on Him. Colossians 1:11 (NCV) tells us, "God will strengthen you with his own great power so that you will not give up when troubles come." I held onto that verse, but I didn't realize that Jesus was getting me ready for more changes.

John completed Step 6—*We were entirely ready to have God remove all these defects of character.* "Humble yourselves before the Lord, and he will lift you up" (James 4:10)—and Step 7—*We humbly asked Him to remove all our shortcomings.* "If we confess our sins, he is faithful and just and will forgive us our sins and purify us from all unrighteousness" (1 John 1:9). He allowed God to change everything in his life and rebuild his self-worth based on God's love for him alone, no longer trying to measure up to the world's standards.

Gradually, John began coming by the house more frequently. He said he was coming to visit the kids, but because they were teenagers, they were often not at home. I began to see a lot of changes in him. He would bring along a pizza or a movie, and we began spending some evenings together. John smiled more often, and sometimes he even laughed out loud. I hadn't seen him laugh like that in years. Although hesitant, Laura and Johnny asked him to join us at our new church. John loved Saddleback Church and said he felt like he was home. He began meeting us there every week on Sunday mornings.

Meanwhile, John began working on Step 8: *We made a list of all persons we had harmed and became willing to make amends to them all.* "Do to others as you would have them do to you" (Luke 6:31). After being separated for a year, John left a note on my table asking me to meet him for lunch.

I was surprised that John wanted to meet for lunch on February 14, 1991 — Valentine's Day! John explained that he was in recovery, and that he went to meetings every day. He was working on Step 9: *We made direct amends to such people whenever possible, except when to do so would injure them or others.* "Therefore, if you are offering your gift at the altar and there remember that your brother has something against you, leave your gift there in front of the altar. First go and be reconciled to your brother; then come and offer your gift" (Matthew 5:23–24).

John told me that he had a lot of names on his amends list, including former employers, employees, friends, and neighbors, but most importantly, he had very special amends to make to Johnny, Laura, and me. He said he was sorry for all of the pain he had caused by his drinking. He took full responsibility for his drinking and freed me from the doubts that I had been the cause of his alcoholism. He said he still loved me, and asked if I would be willing to work on the marriage.

God changed our lives with Step 9. John and I began to work on the issues that had torn apart our marriage. We made Step 10 a part of our daily lives: *We continued to take personal inventory and when we were wrong promptly admitted it.* "So, if you think you are standing firm, be careful that you don't fall!" (1 Corinthians 10:12).

Five months after John's ninth step to me, God opened our hearts and we renewed our wedding vows. As a family, we were baptized together, and we took all of the church's membership classes together. In the maturity class, John found one of his life's verses, 1 Peter 2:9–10 (TLB): "You have been chosen by God himself ... you are the priest of the King ... you are God's very own—all this so you can show to others how God called you out of the darkness into his wonderful light. Once you were less than nothing; now you are God's very own."

However, at John's secular meetings, some of the men made fun of him whenever he talked about his higher power, the one and only true Higher Power, Jesus. It seemed as though anything could be claimed as a higher power, just not Jesus. At church, we tried to find a small group where we could be open and honest about the issues that had torn our marriage apart. But we couldn't find that safe place—a group of other Christians who wanted to share openly about their struggles.

We began working Step 11: *We sought through prayer and meditation to improve our conscious contact with God, praying only for knowledge of His will for us and power to carry that out.* "Let the message of Christ dwell in you richly" (Colossians 3:16). Finally, John said, "We can't be this different from everyone at church. We can't be the only ones struggling with a hurt, hang-up, or habit." At the time, Saddleback Church had over 6,000 members.

John began writing down an outline for a program that would fit our needs. Realizing that "God never wastes a hurt," the pain and the heartache of his sin addiction to alcohol were finally beginning to have a purpose. In Joel 2:25, God promises to restore "the years the locusts have eaten." We discussed the ideas for the program for weeks while the vision from God continued to grow. We saw an opportunity to share our hurts with others as we began to work Step 12: *Having had a spiritual experience as a result of these steps, we try to carry this message to others and to practice these principles in all our affairs.* "Brothers, if someone is caught in a sin, you who are spiritual should restore him gently. But watch yourself, or you also may be tempted" (Galatians 6:1).

John finally finished a thirteen-page, single-spaced letter for a vision of a ministry called Celebrate Recovery—a Christ-centered recovery program. In summary, the letter said, "The vision for Celebrate Recovery is for the church to provide a safe place where families could find healing and restoration; where moms, dads, and their children of all ages could find freedom from their hurts, hang-ups, and habits."

John gave the letter to Rick Warren, the senior pastor of Saddleback Church. We were confident that Rick would find just the right godly man to head up this new ministry. Neither of us was prepared for Rick to call John into his office and say, "It's a great idea, John, I would like you to do it!"

The first meeting for Celebrate Recovery started on November 21, 1991. Saddleback Church did not have any property, so the only place we could find to hold our meeting was a psychiatric hospital! And, still, God used it—forty-three people attended! In order for the whole family to be able to come, we provided child care. Our son and daughter, Johnny and Laura, started the open share group for teens. A small group of volunteers led our worship, and the lessons were taught in a large group format. Since at that point we did not have any recovery stories from our program, we did not have testimonies. As time went on, testimonies were added to our large group as people began to want to share how Jesus Christ was changing their lives.

There were four groups: a woman's chemical addiction, a men's codependent, a men's chemical addiction (led by John), and a woman's codependent (led by me). I didn't even know what a codependent was! But I wanted to share with others who could identify with our struggles, so I was willing to learn.

After the meetings were over, we were all so excited to talk about our recoveries with other Christians that we went to a restaurant to keep sharing. Often we would close down the restaurant, and then go back to our house so that we could continue our conversations. It was such a relief to talk to others who understood our hurts, hang-ups, and habits. We had found a safe place; we were no longer different or alone.

This program was working for our family and that is all we hoped to accomplish. We just needed to keep the program going. But God had so many other plans! John was asked to join the Saddleback Church staff in 1992. He served at Celebrate Recovery as a volunteer while his job was to oversee the small ministries of the church.

In 1993, because lives were changing at Celebrate Recovery, Rick decided to take the entire church through "The Road to Recovery" sermon series of the eight principles based on the Beatitudes. This series helped us to experience another growing phase. But more importantly, Celebrate Recovery participants began to serve in other areas of the church. While finally experiencing freedom and forgiveness, and with many tears, Celebrate Recovery even served communion. Saddleback Church became a safe place for anyone with a hurt.

In order to better understand the choices that we had made in our lives, we began to feel that we needed something in addition to the open share groups. We decided to try some of the Christian 12-Step published materials. Often we would start off a group of twenty-five men or women, but only two or three would finish the study. The available, published resources did not work for us.

So the search began for a Christian study that was based on the Bible and would apply to anyone with a hurt, hang-up, or habit. We wanted the curriculum to be concise and easy to use while helping people deal with their past in a thorough manner. We studied many resources, but none of them seemed to be a good fit for Celebrate Recovery.

As the search continued for the right curriculum, our participants were having trouble getting through Step 4. John slowed down the lessons and took three months to teach on that principle. At the completion of those lessons, many had completed the step successfully and were ready to move on in their recovery. One of the leaders, Carl, was so impressed with John's teaching, that he suggested he put his teaching notes into a fourth step workbook.

Not having much confidence in his writing abilities, John quickly said he would consider the idea but within a few days had forgotten all about the request. However, as John would arrive at the next Celebrate Recovery meeting, Carl would greet him at the door and ask how the fourth step workbook was coming along. He repeated the same scenario at the Saturday night and Sunday church services. "How's that fourth step workbook coming?"

John finally decided that God was using Carl to encourage him to write the workbook, so he completed the participant's guide in 1994. The book was based on God's Word, so it was not addiction or compulsion based. We knew that it worked because the lessons had been so successful at Celebrate Recovery, and it applied to anyone with a hurt, hang-up, or habit.

Since Saddleback is a teaching church, it was not long before several churches in California were using the workbook. Then some churches in other states began incorporating the book into their programs. Much to our surprise, Canada and Australia contacted us about using this fourth step workbook. The workbook was helping people from all over the world get through their fourth step. Carl had been right.

And then it wasn't long before John began getting requests for the workbooks for steps one through three and steps five through twelve. All of a sudden, John had hundreds of "Carls" all over the country asking for step study workbooks. He went back to the computer and the late nights and completed all four workbooks—the participant's guides—in 1995. The workbooks included all twelve steps and the eight principles. Finally, the search for a Celebrate Recovery curriculum was over.

As we began to use the participant's guides, we had a huge

growth spurt. Leaders began to emerge from those step study groups and wanted to start new groups. Gradually, groups for newcomers, anger, eating disorders, food addiction, love and relationship addiction, sexual addiction, codependents in a relationship with a sexually addicted man, gambling, sexual/physical/emotional abuse, and adult children of the chemically addicted were added to the original four small groups.

The participant's guides began to be shipped all over the country, and people started calling the church office to find out how to start Celebrate Recovery at their churches. The questions were endless and complex. "How do you start the program? How do you find leaders? How can you prepare lessons with full-time jobs and family commitments?" In order to answer the flood of questions, a leader's guide was written in 1996.

For a couple of years, John and I printed those participant's guides and leader's guides and sold them from our garage. We had a post office box for the orders. It was a highlight of our week to pick up the orders and learn where Celebrate Recovery programs were being started. This Christ-centered recovery program was beginning to appear all over the United States, and other countries were starting the program as well!

In 1998, in order for the participant's guides and the leader's guide to receive wider distribution, Zondervan took over printing and distributing the materials. The participant's guides and leader's guide have now been published in twenty-three different languages and are in forty-five prison systems. Luke 4:18 (MSG) says, "God's spirit is on me; he's chosen me to preach the Message of good news to the poor, sent me to announce pardon to prisoners and recovery of sight to the blind, to set the burdened and the battered free ..."

As the program continued, Celebrate Recovery leaders from across the country wanted to meet one another and to develop a network. In 1999, the first Celebrate Recovery Summit was held at Saddleback Church for that purpose and seventy-three people attended. Twelve years later, a sold-out crowd of 3,400 people met at Saddleback Church to learn how to meet the growing numbers of people with hurts, hang-ups, and habits. The network now includes regional and international directors, a prison director, and volunteer state representatives who help Celebrate Recovery programs get started and continue to grow. This was beyond our wildest dreams!

Celebrate Recovery began as a ministry at Saddleback Church so that our family could have a safe place to share the struggles that had torn us apart. We wanted to identify with others who would claim Jesus Christ as their Higher Power and were willing to turn their lives completely over to Him.

Now our "Forever Family" includes people from all over the world who want to break the cycle of dysfunction and live out 2 Corinthians 1:3–4 with us: "Praise be to the God and Father of our Lord Jesus Christ, the Father of compassion and the God of all comfort, who comforts us in all our troubles, so that we can comfort those in any trouble with the comfort we ourselves receive from God."

Victory Can Be Yours As Well

I hope you can see from Cheryl's testimony how God changed two broken lives and restored our marriage so that we could live out God's purpose in Celebrate Recovery. It is our prayer that you will read the rest of this book with an open heart, knowing everyone has hurts, hang-ups, or habits. One of the misconceptions about the word *recovery* is that it is only for those struggling with drugs and alcohol. Of over the million people who have gone through a Celebrate Recovery step study, only one out of three has been dealing with substance abuse.

The remainder of the book is designed to remove any fears, doubts, or questions you might have about attending a Celebrate Recovery meeting for the first time.

If you are going through any type of hurt, hang-up, or habit, Celebrate Recovery is for you.

God can give you the same victory He has given us!

Chapter 2

How Do I
Know Celebrate
Recovery Works?

Change Is Possible: The Eight Principles of Celebrate Recovery

Since the beginning of time, men and women have searched for happiness—usually in all the wrong places, trying all the wrong things. But there's only one place where we can find tested-and-proven, absolutely-gonna-work principles that will lead to healing and happiness. These principles come in the form of eight statements from the truest of all books—the Bible—and from the most revered Teacher of all time—Jesus Christ. Jesus laid out these principles for happiness in the Sermon on the Mount in the gospel of Matthew, chapter 5. Today we call them "the Beatitudes."

Change, Jesus says, can be ours, but the pathway to change and happiness may not be exactly what we're expecting. From a conventional viewpoint, most of the following eight statements don't make sense. At first they even sound like contradictions. But when you fully understand what Jesus is saying, you'll realize these eight statements are God's pathway to wholeness, growth, and spiritual maturity.

"Happy are those who know they are spiritually poor."
"Happy are those who mourn, for they shall be comforted."
"Happy are the meek."
"Happy are the pure in heart."
*"Happy are those whose greatest desire is to do what God
    requires."*
"Happy are those who are merciful."
"Happy are those who work for peace."
*"Happy are those who are persecuted because they do what God
    requires."**

My Own Personal Journey

I know that the eight principles work. Why? Because they worked
in my life. I have not always been a pastor. Prior to being called into
the ministry, I was a successful businessman. I was also a "func-
tional alcoholic." My wife Cheryl told my story in chapter one. I
struggled with my sin addiction to alcohol for nineteen years. Eventually I came to a point where I was losing everything. I cried out to
God for help, and He led me to Alcoholics Anonymous. Even then
I knew that my Higher Power had a name—Jesus Christ! I started
attending Saddleback Church in Lake Forest, California. After a
year of sobriety, God gave me the vision for Celebrate Recovery, a
Christ-centered recovery program. I answered God's call to start
Celebrate Recovery. Since 1991, over a million courageous individuals have found the same freedom from their life's hurts, hang-ups,
and habits that I did. If these eight principles worked for someone
like me, I promise they can work for you too!

My Partnership with Pastor Rick

After Celebrate Recovery had been going for a year, Pastor Rick
Warren, my senior pastor, saw how Celebrate Recovery was helping people in our church family find God's healing from their

---

* All quotations of the Beatitudes throughout this book are taken
from the *Good News Translation (Today's English Version).*

Principles That Will Change Your Life

The Road to Recovery
Based on the Beatitudes
Pastor Rick Warren

PRINCIPLE 1	**R**ealize I'm not God. I admit that I am powerless to control my tendency to do the wrong thing and that my life is unmanageable (Step 1). *"Happy are those who know they are spiritually poor"* (Matthew 5:3).
PRINCIPLE 2	**E**arnestly believe that God exists, that I matter to Him, and that He has the power to help me recover (Step 2). *"Happy are those who mourn, for they shall be comforted"* (Matthew 5:4).
PRINCIPLE 3	**C**onsciously choose to commit all my life and will to Christ's care and control (Step 3). *"Happy are the meek"* (Matthew 5:5).
PRINCIPLE 4	**O**penly examine and confess my faults to myself, to God, and to someone I trust (Steps 4 and 5). *"Happy are the pure in heart"* (Matthew 5:8).
PRINCIPLE 5	**V**oluntarily submit to every change God wants to make in my life and humbly ask Him to remove my character defects (Steps 6 and 7). *"Happy are those whose greatest desire is to do what God requires"* (Matthew 5:6).
PRINCIPLE 6	**E**valuate all my relationships. Offer forgiveness to those who have hurt me and make amends for harm I've done to others, except when to do so would harm them or others (Steps 8 and 9). *"Happy are the merciful"* (Matthew 5:7). *"Happy are the peacemakers"* (Matthew 5:9).
PRINCIPLE 7	**R**eserve a daily time with God for self-examination, Bible reading, and prayer in order to know God and His will for my life and to gain the power to follow His will (Steps 10 and 11).
PRINCIPLE 8	**Y**ield myself to God to be used to bring this Good News to others, both by my example and by my words (Step 12). *"Happy are those who are persecuted because they do what God requires"* (Matthew 5:10).

hurts, hang-ups, and habits. He decided to take the entire church family through a sermon series called "The Road to Recovery."

Pastor Rick's R-E-C-O-V-E-R-Y acrostic identifies eight principles. As you read the eight principles and the corresponding beatitudes (see box on page 29), you'll begin to understand the choices before you. (Throughout this chapter, you also will be introduced to the Christ-centered 12 Steps. These have been adapted from the 12 Suggested Steps of Alcoholics Anonymous, with the significant difference that we know our Higher Power to be Jesus Christ. To read these Steps and their biblical comparisons in one convenient spot, please see Appendix A on page 119.)

We will explore each of the eight Celebrate Recovery principles in the rest of this chapter. Let's begin with Principle 1. (NOTE: After four of the eight principles—4, 5, 7, and 8—you'll find a personal story, a testimony by a real person from the Celebrate Recovery family. You will see how with God's power, and working their program, they are overcoming their hurts, hang-ups, and habits. These courageous individuals come from very different backgrounds with a variety of problems and issues. As you read their stories, please keep your heart and mind open. You will see how their journeys relate to your own life or to someone's close to you.)

Principle 1

> **Principle 1:** Realize I'm not God. I admit that I am powerless to control my tendency to do the wrong thing and that my life is unmanageable.
>
> *"Happy are those who know they are spiritually poor." (Matthew 5:3)*

Your amazing recovery journey starts with Principle 1, where you admit that you are powerless to control your hurts, hang-ups, and habits and that your life has become unmanageable, out of control. But before you begin this exciting journey, you need to ask yourself the following two questions:

Am I wearing a mask of denial?
Over what do I really have control?

These questions are not just for you, but for everyone! Let's look at the first question: Are we wearing a mask of denial? Before we can make any progress in our recovery, we need to face our denial. As soon as we remove our mask, our recovery begins — or begins again! It doesn't matter whether someone is new in recovery or they have been in the process and working the principles and steps for years. Denial can rear its ugly head and return at any time. We may trade addictions or get into a new relationship that's unhealthy for us in a different way than a previous one.

God says in Jeremiah 6:14 (TLB), "You can't heal a wound by saying it's not there."

Denial is serious. We can't heal our hurts, hang-ups, and habits by pretending they're not there. Denial will disable our feelings, isolating us from God and alienating us from others.

As soon as we start working on this principle and admit that we're powerless, we begin to change. We see that our old ways of trying to control our hurts, hang-ups, and habits didn't work. Our attempts were buried by our denial, and our problems were held close by our false sense of power.

This leads us to the second question we need to answer: Over what do we really have control? In Principle 1 we recognize our need to admit our powerlessness. Our lust for the power to control is rooted in our weaknesses, not in our strengths. We need to realize our human weaknesses and turn our lives over to God. Jesus knew this would be difficult. How difficult? He said this about a related issue, but it applies here as well: "With man this is impossible, but with God all things are possible" (Matthew 19:26).

Pride, worry, resentment, selfishness, and loneliness act like "serenity robbers" in our lives. We have to come to a place where we admit that we are powerless.

The power to change comes only from God's grace. In Principle 1 we start working and living this program in earnest. When we admit we're powerless, we go on to recognize that we need a power greater than ourselves to restore us. That power is the one and only true Higher Power, Jesus Christ.

Hebrews 12:1 invites us: "Therefore, since we are surrounded by such a great cloud of witnesses, let us throw off everything that hinders and the sin that so easily entangles. And let us run with perseverance the race marked out for us."

This verse spells out two important insights as we begin our recovery journey. First, God has a particular race, a unique plan, for each of us—a plan for good, not a life consumed with dependencies, addictions, and obsessions. The second thing is that we need to be willing to get rid of all the unnecessary baggage— hurts, hang-ups, and habits—in our lives that keep us stuck ("let us throw off everything that hinders and the sin that so easily entangles"). Working through the eight principles will allow us to discover God's plan and purpose for our lives. The journey begins by taking the first step.

The first step of the Christ-centered 12 Steps relates to Principle 1:

Step 1: We admitted we were powerless over our addictions and compulsive behaviors, that our lives had become unmanageable.

"I know that nothing good lives in me, that is, in my sinful nature. For I have the desire to do what is good, but I cannot carry it out."
(Romans 7:18)

Principle 1 Prayer

Dear God, Your Word tells me that I can't heal my hurts, hang-ups, and habits just by saying they're not there. Help me! Parts of my life—or all of my life—are out of control. I now know that I can't "fix" myself. It seems that the harder I try to do the right thing, the more I struggle. Lord, I want to step out of my denial into the truth. I pray for you to show me the way. In your Son's name, Amen.

Principle 2

> **Principle 2:** Earnestly believe that God exists, that I matter to Him, and that He has the power to help me recover.
>
> *"Happy are those who mourn, for they will be comforted."*
> *(Matthew 5:4)*

In Principle 2 you will find the power for your recovery as you earnestly believe that God exists, that you matter to Him, and that He has the power to help you recover.

Hebrews 11:6 tells us, "Without faith it is impossible to please God, because anyone who comes to him must believe that he exists and that he rewards those who earnestly seek him." And Psalm 62:5 invites, "Yes, my soul, find rest in God; my hope comes from him."

In the first principle, we admitted that we're powerless. It's through this admission that we're able to *believe* and *receive* God's power to help us recover. We do need to be careful, though, not to cover up the pit of our hurts, hang-ups, and habits with layers of denial or to try some quick "fix." Instead, we need to expose our hurts, hang-ups, and habits to the light so that through God's power we can truly find healing.

In the second principle, we come to believe that God exists, that we're important to Him, and that we're able to find the one true Higher Power, Jesus Christ. We come to understand that God wants to fill our lives with His love, joy, and presence.

In Luke 15:11 – 32 we find the parable of the lost son. This story about a father's love for his wayward son is really a picture of the love of God the Father for all of us. God's love is looking for us no matter how lost we may feel. God's searching love can find us no matter how many times we may have fallen into sin. God's hands of mercy are reaching out to pick us up, to love us, and to forgive us. He is the only place where we'll find hope.

The second step of the Christ-centered 12 Steps relates to Principle 2.

Step 2: We came to believe that a power greater than ourselves could restore us to sanity.

"For it is God who works in you to will and to act according to his good purpose." (Philippians 2:13)

In this principle we come to believe that a power greater than ourselves can help us recover—can restore us to sanity. This isn't to say we're crazy. The word *sanity* in this context means that as a result of admitting our powerlessness in Principle 1, we can move from chaos into hope in Principle 2. Hope comes when we believe that a power greater than ourselves, our Higher Power, Jesus Christ, can and will restore us. Jesus alone can provide that power, since on our own we are powerless over our hurts, hang-ups, and destructive habits. He alone can restore order and meaning to our lives. He alone can restore us to sanity.

A working definition of *insanity* in this context might be doing the same thing over and over again but expecting a different result each time.

Sanity, using this model, may, on the other hand, be defined as "wholeness of mind; making decisions based on the truth."

Jesus is the only Higher Power who offers the truth, as well as the power, the way, and the life.

We can't follow through with anything unless and until we get started. But just how much faith do we need to start working this principle? Jesus provides the answer in Matthew 17:20: "I tell you the truth, if you have faith as small as a mustard seed, you can say to this mountain, 'Move from here to there' and it will move. Nothing will be impossible for you."

It's reassuring to know that we don't need large doses of faith as we begin the recovery process. We need only a little faith, as small as the tiniest of seeds, to effect change, to begin to move away our mountains of hurts, hang-ups, and habits.

Eternal life doesn't begin with death; it begins with faith. Hebrews 11:1 explains what faith is: "Faith is being sure of what we hope for and certain of what we do not see." We can't find salvation through intellectual understanding, monetary gifts, good works, or church attendance. The way—the only way—to find salvation is described in Romans 10:9: "If you confess with your mouth, 'Jesus is Lord,' and believe in your heart that God raised him from the dead, you will be saved."

We'll find our true hope in the only Higher Power, Jesus Christ. As we take this step of hope, his Spirit will come with supernatural power to reside in our hearts. The Holy Spirit will give us the courage to reach out and take hold of Christ's hand, to face the present with confidence and the future with realistic expectancy.

Simply put, life without Christ is a hopeless end; with him life is an endless hope.

Principle 2 Prayer

Dear God, I've tried hard to fix and control my life's hurts, hang-ups, and habits. I admit that, by myself, I'm powerless to change. I need to begin to believe and receive Your power to help me recover. You loved me enough to send Your Son to the cross to die for my sins. Help me to open myself up to the hope I can find only in Jesus. Please help me to start living my life in reliance upon this hope, one day at a time. In Jesus' name I pray, Amen.

Principle 3

Principle 3: Consciously choose to commit all my life and will to Christ's care and control.

"Happy are the meek." (Matthew 5:5)

In Principle 3 you will make the one-time, permanent decision to turn over your life to the care of God—the most important decision you'll ever make. Your choice, not chance, determines your destiny. And that decision requires only putting your faith into action.

But what is faith? It isn't a sense, sight, or reason. Faith is simply taking God at His word. As we learned in Principle 2, God's Word tells us in Romans 10:9 that "if you declare with your mouth, 'Jesus is Lord,' and believe in your heart that God raised him from the dead, you will be saved." For some people that seems just too simple. But it isn't. Our salvation depends much more on God's love for us than on our love for him.

Many people don't understand that putting off the decision to accept Jesus Christ as their Higher Power, as their Lord and Savior, is really deciding not to accept him. Principle 3 is like opening the door: All you need is the willingness to make the decision. Christ will do the rest. He calls out to us, "Here I am! I stand at the door and knock. If anyone hears my voice and opens the door, I will come in and eat with that person, and they with me" (Revelation 3:20).

If we're going to successfully work Principle 3, we need to get past our old, familiar, negative barriers of pride, fear, guilt, worry, and doubt. But how do we break this cycle? The answer is that we need to be proactive, to take the initiative. In fact, Principle 3 is all about action.

Turning over our lives to Christ is a one-time, yet permanent, commitment. Once we accept Christ as Lord of our life, it's a done deal. We can't lose our salvation. It comes with a lifetime (in this case, eternal) guarantee from the Holy Spirit: "You also were included in Christ when you heard the message of truth, the gospel of your salvation. When you believed, you were marked in him with a seal, the promised Holy Spirit" (Ephesians 1:13).

The rest of the principle, though—the part about turning over our wills to Christ—requires a daily recommitment. We can begin by going to our Bible regularly, opening it prayerfully, reading it expectantly, and living it joyfully.

The third step of the Christ-centered 12 Steps relates to Principle 3.

Step 3: We made a decision to turn our lives and our wills over to the care of God.

"Therefore, I urge you, brothers, in view of God's mercy, to offer your bodies as living sacrifices, holy and pleasing to God—this is your spiritual act of worship." (Romans 12:1)

Principle 3 states that we choose to commit our lives and wills to Christ's care. In the secular 12 Steps, Step 3 gets the sequence confused, telling us to "turn our wills and our lives over ..." The fact is that we must first commit and surrender our lives to the one and only true Higher Power, Jesus Christ. Then and only then are we empowered to turn over our *wills* to Him.

Principle 3 constitutes the core difference between a secular 12-Step program and Celebrate Recovery. True and lasting recovery can be achieved only through a personal, committed relationship with Christ.

In the secular 12 Steps, Step 3 is: "We made a decision to turn our wills and our lives over to the care of God, as we understand him." But we need a God much, much greater than anything that stems from our own imagination or understanding. We need the one true God, the Almighty, the Creator of the universe. First Corinthians 13:12 tells us, "Now we see only a reflection as in a mirror; then we shall see face to face. Now I know in part; then I shall know fully, even as I am fully known." Someday we'll see Jesus face to face. The fog of interpretation will be lifted, and our understanding will be perfected.

Praise God that we don't need a complete understanding of Jesus in order to ask Him into our lives as Lord and Savior. Why? Because God does more than lead us day by day and year by year. He directs our way moment by moment, one step after another.

If you haven't asked Jesus Christ to be your Higher Power, the Lord and Savior of your life, what are you waiting for? All it takes is praying this prayer with a sincere heart:

Principle 3 Prayer

Dear God, I've tried—and failed—to do it all by myself in my own power. Today I want to turn my life over to You. I ask You to be my Lord and Savior. You're the one and only Higher Power. I ask You to help me think less about myself and my own will. I want to turn over my will, moment by moment, to You, to continuously seek Your direction and wisdom for my life. Please continue to help me overcome my hurts, hang-ups, and habits, so that victory over them may help others as they see Your power at work in my already changed, and still changing, life. Help me to do Your will always. In Jesus' name I pray, Amen.

Principle 4

Principle 4: Openly examine and confess my faults to myself, to God, and to someone I trust.

"Happy are the pure in heart." (Matthew 5:8)

Principle 4 begins the process of "coming clean." It's here that you openly examine and confess your faults to yourself, to God, and to another person you trust. You begin to chip away at the "truth decay" of your past. The negative effects of your hurts, hang-ups, and habits have built up, like a layer of tartar, over the years and have kept you from really seeing the truth about your past and present situations.

In the first part of this principle, we need to "openly examine" our faults. We need to list, or inventory, all of the significant events—both good and bad—in our lives. We need to be as honest as we can in order to allow God to show us our part in each event and how that has affected both ourselves and others. We need to do a searching and fearless inventory, to step out of our denial, because we can't put our faults behind us until we've faced them. We need to see through our denial of the past into the truth of the present—to identify our true feelings, motives, and thoughts.

Our inventory brings us to a black-and-white discovery of who we really are at our core. But if we look only at the bad parts of our past, we distort our inventory and open ourselves up to unnecessary pain. Lamentations 3:40 invites us, "Let us examine our ways and test them, and let us return to the LORD." Notice that the verse doesn't say, "Examine your bad, negative ways." We need to honestly focus on both the positives and the negatives of our past.

We accomplish that by taking a MORAL inventory. That word *moral* scares some people. But at its root, it simply means "honest."

In this principle, we list the people we resent or fear, the specific actions others have taken to hurt us, the ways in which those hurtful actions have affected our lives, and the wrongs or injuries we've inflicted on others.

This is done by taking a Spiritual Inventory. Through this process, we examine eight key areas of our lives:

Our relationships with others—Matthew 6:12–14
Our priorities in life—Matthew 6:33
Our attitude—Ephesians 4:31
Our integrity—Colossians 3:9
Our mind—Romans 12:2
Our body—1 Corinthians 6:19–20
Our family—Joshua 24:15
Our church—Hebrews 10:25

The fourth step of the Christ-centered 12 Steps relates to the first part of Principle 4.

Step 4: We made a searching and fearless moral inventory of ourselves.

> *"Let us examine our ways and test them, and let us return to the LORD." (Lamentations 3:40)*

As soon as we complete our inventories in the first part of Principle 4, we need to confess our faults to ourselves, to God, and to someone else we trust. After we share our inventories—the good and bad things of our past and present—we'll find the peace and freedom for which we may have been searching our entire lives. We need to confess our shortcomings, resentments, and sins. God wants us to come clean, to admit that wrong is wrong, that we're "guilty as charged."

In confession we agree with God regarding our sins, and our fellowship with Him is restored. Principle 4 sums up how we go about obeying God's direction in confessing our sins: First, we confessed our sins to God so we could be forgiven. Then we confessed them to another person we trust so we could start the healing process.

The fifth step of the Christ-centered 12 Steps relates to this part of Principle 4.

Step 5: We admitted to God, to ourselves, and to another human being the exact nature of our wrongs.

> *"Therefore confess your sins to each other and pray for each other so that you may be healed." (James 5:16)*

Some people feel that if they ADMIT their sins to another they have everything to lose and nothing to gain. The following is the truth about four things we have to lose and three things we have to gain by sharing our inventories with someone we trust:

We lose:

1. *Our sense of isolation.* Our feeling of aloneness will begin to vanish.
2. *Our unwillingness to forgive.* When people accept and forgive us, we start to see that we, in turn, can forgive others.
3. *Our inflated, false pride.* As we realistically see and accept ourselves, we begin to gain true humility, which involves seeing ourselves as we really are and God as He really is.
4. *Our sense of denial.* Being truthful with another person begins to tear away at our denial. We begin to feel clean and honest.

We gain:

1. *Healing that the Bible promises.* Look again at James 5:16. The key word here is *healed*. Notice that the verse doesn't say, "Confess your sins to one another and you will be forgiven," although we hope this will be so, at least in terms of the other person. God already forgave us when we confessed our sins to Him. Now He promises that we'll begin the healing process when we confess our sins to someone else.
2. *Freedom.* Our secrets have kept us in chains—bound, frozen, unable to move forward in any of our relationships, either with God or with others. Admitting our sins snaps the chains so God's healing power can be released.
3. *Support.* When we share our inventory with another person, we gain support. Our accountability partner can help us stay focused and provide valuable feedback.

An important part of Celebrate Recovery is for each of us to have accountability relationships. Don't attempt to work through this fourth principle alone. We need sponsors and/or accountability partners of the same gender for the following three reasons:

1. Having someone fill this role for us is a key part of our recovery program.

By walking alongside us on the road to recovery, a sponsor

and/or an accountability partner keeps us on track as we complete the eight principles.

Proverbs 20:5 says: "The purposes of a person's heart are deep waters, but one who has insight draws them out." We need a man or woman who understands us as an individual and who also understands what we're going through in order to help us in our recovery.

2. Having a sponsor and/or an accountability partner is biblical.

Ecclesiastes 4:9 – 10 tells us: "Two are better than one, because they have a good return for their labor: If either of them falls down, one can help the other up. But pity anyone who falls and has no one to help them up."

And Proverbs 27:17 points out: "As iron sharpens iron, so one person sharpens another." The phrase *one another* is used in the New Testament over fifty times.

3. Having a sponsor and/or an accountability partner is the best guard against relapse.

By providing feedback to keep us on track, a sponsor and/or an accountability partner can see our old dysfunctional, self-defeating patterns beginning to resurface and quickly point them out to us. This person can confront us in a spirit of truth and love without piling on shame or guilt.

Ecclesiastes 7:5 states: "It is better to heed the rebuke of a wise person than to listen to the song of fools." The trouble with most of us is that we'd rather be ruined by praise than saved by criticism.

As we complete Principle 4, we need to remember that no matter how bad our past actions may have been, we can hold on to the assurance offered by Romans 8:1: "Therefore, there is now no condemnation for those who are in Christ Jesus."

Principle 4 can be summed up in one verse, Isaiah 1:18: " 'Come now, let us settle the matter,' says the LORD. 'Though your sins are like scarlet, they shall be as white as snow; though they are red as crimson, they shall be like wool.' "

Principle 4 Prayer

Dear God, You know our past; You're familiar with all the good and bad things we've done. In this principle, we ask You to give us the strength and courage to list them so we can "come clean" and face both our past and the truth about our present and future. Please help us reach out to those special persons You've placed along our road to recovery. Thank You for providing them to help us maintain balance as we work on our inventories. In Christ's name I pray, Amen.

PRINCIPLE 4 TESTIMONY

My name is Marnie, and I am a grateful believer in Jesus Christ who struggles with sexual addiction and food issues.

I wish I could start this story "Once upon a time" or "There once was a little girl." But instead it starts like this: A broken home, tortuous abuse, fits of rage, and being stripped away from those I held dear to my heart. And this was just a fraction of my childhood that began my forbidden lifestyle filled with fantasy, sex, and lust.

My path to recovery started at Saddleback Church in November of 2000. I remember that night well. I crawled in broken and completely unaware of reality. My view on life had become so distorted and my actions had become so out of control, I don't think the enemy himself could've kept up.

That night I watched as people smiled, hugged, and celebrated, because it happened to be the ninth anniversary of Celebrate Recovery. I arrived an hour early, completely unaware that the worship service didn't start until seven o'clock. So, I sat and listened to the band rehearse.

I remember sitting there, *almost* all alone, with only a handful of people walking around setting things up. As I looked around, tears began to form in my eyes and it was all I could do to blink them back. I didn't know what I was doing there. My thoughts were wandering and had become so disjointed. Everything within me wanted to just get up and walk out. It was evident I was still in denial. I kept hearing the same thoughts repeating themselves in my head: *Whatever is wrong with these people is way worse than anything I could have done!* and *Whatever I've done, I'm sure I can fix it on my own!* But for some reason I just could not bring myself to get up out of that chair and leave.

I was startled as a man came up to me, put his hand on my shoulder, and said, "Excuse me, but this seat is taken." As I looked around the empty room, it took me a while to realize that he was kidding. But you know, just in those few words, I felt a sense of comfort and relief. I felt welcomed and a little less "out of place."

That night I attended Newcomers 101 where, for the first time, I confessed my secrets. I managed to utter the words that had gone unspoken for years— *"I cheated on my husband"*—and moments after that, I began to sob. That was it. That was all I said. The woman, who was leading 101 that night, leaned forward, cupped my hands in hers and told me for the first time "Everything's going to be okay. You've come to the right place." The sincerity in her voice warmed me.

Long before I was born, there was already turmoil brewing in my family. Before my first birthday, my parents had finalized their plan to divorce. My older sister and I were sent to live with my father and grandparents in Hawaii. Once we arrived, my dad conveniently left the scene. My grandparents were unofficially assigned to care for us as if we were their own. My fondest childhood memories are of the years I spent with my grandparents in Hawaii. They taught me about Jesus, and by their example, I learned Christian values. Thankfully, they showed me what it was like to live in a "normal" family. My parents, on the other hand, were diabolical opposites of my grandparents.

My father is a functioning alcoholic, who also has a wandering eye for women. I watched as my dad moved from relationship to relationship and as his addiction to pornography and alcohol grew. His complete disregard for his calling as a father allowed me plenty of time to explore as a young child. I can remember being crouched in a corner with my sister as we attempted to smoke cigarettes and drink some of my dad's beer. As a young girl, curiosity took me by surprise one day when I was snooping around the house and found my dad's *Playboy* collection hidden in his dresser drawers. I felt as though I had just stumbled upon a secret, and I ran out of the room. But at the same time, I was intrigued at the images I saw. Often, my dad would take my sister and me to his girlfriend's house where we were abandoned in the living room and told to watch television while Dad retreated into the bedroom with his girlfriend. Even at such a young age, I was well aware of what they were doing. I viewed this as a totally acceptable lifestyle. My last encounter with my father was when I was in my twenties. That day I wandered onto his patio to find an enraged, drunken man waving a butcher knife in my face.

At the age of five, I moved back to California to live with my mother. She has the personality of a raging alcoholic, minus the alcohol. The movie *Mommy Dearest* comes to mind. She was physically, verbally, and emotionally abusive. One unpleasant incident that sticks with me the most was when I was packing to go on a camping trip with family friends. I walked in on her in one of her fits of rage and she slapped me in the face so hard that my tooth punctured my lip. Needless to say, I had a huge fat lip and black eye the following day. I told everyone I had been eating and that my fork had slipped. She'd always apologize and say she hated what she had done, but in the next breath tell me I deserved it. I don't know how many times I ended up in the hospital as a young girl. I remember vividly my mother being sent out of the room and the doctors asking, "Did your mother hit you?" and with a stoic face, my response always being a simple shake of the head "no."

Throughout my childhood, I became my mother's human piñata—often a victim of choking and dodging mirrors she threw at me. I also was beaten with lamps, hangers, high-heeled shoes, and whatever else was within reach. To cope with my dysfunctional life, I escaped into a fantasy life, filled with lustful thoughts and pornographic images that were embedded in my mind. I would stay in bed for hours fanaticizing about sexual acts, replaying the same dreams over and over again in my head.

My upbringing was so filled with turmoil that I had no choice but to escape the insanity. Just before the start of my senior year of high school, I emancipated myself. At seventeen, legally, I was recognized as an adult. I moved out and was on my own. I was determined to break the cycle of dysfunction I had been living with all of my life. But I had become a product of my environment.

I married my high school sweetheart in June of '98. Marriage started off difficult for us. Although we had dated for eight years prior to getting married, it almost seemed that, in an instant we had grown miles apart, as if our years together had somehow been reversed. Our conversations were no longer familiar. Instead, we stuck to superficial topics. Hard times were beginning to materialize. We were struggling financially and we were living with his parents. The enemy sank his fangs into me as I viewed my marriage as a mistake; a "verbal blunder," so to speak; a prison. Bitterness, resentment, and hatred started to paint an ugly picture, as my visions of a "normal" lifestyle fell by the wayside. We went through months of arguing and a lot of broken promises. I felt like I was running in place. I felt taken advantage of, disrespected, and unappreciated. I felt like I had no voice and no control. I felt robbed of my dreams. Most of all, I felt emotionally bankrupt. It was then that my behavior exploded into an uncontrollable fury; my solution, adultery. Just ten short months into my marriage, I had cheated on my husband.

As my addictive lifestyle was starting to take shape, I took a new position at work, which would require me to fly to the Bay Area every Monday and fly home every Thursday. All of this free time away from my husband gave me the freedom to make my own choices, which only fueled my unhealthy behaviors. In my denial, life never felt so good. I was getting attention from men I hardly knew and who hardly knew me. Every day, I became more and more independent of my marriage. I felt in control. I was finally doing something I thought I wanted to do instead of having to live by someone else's rules. But in my heart, I knew something was desperately wrong. I struggled with confusion about the Christian values I had been taught as a child versus what the world deems as socially acceptable behavior. I suddenly felt as if I only knew these childhood beliefs intellectually. For the first time in my life, my faith in God had been tried and shaken, because at this point in my life, my relationship with the Lord was nonexistent. I ignored those feelings and instead replaced them with alcohol, anorexia, and adultery. I was now on a suicide mission *"devoted to a life of deception."* My life became intertwined with the very women I had been warned against in my childhood teachings of the Bible: Jezebel, Potiphar's wife, and Delilah. My life had now become a reflection of the woman whose *"greatest accomplishment in life was the destruction of the man who loved her most."* My forbidden lifestyle progressed into a double life. I continued keeping up the variety of appearances that had sustained me throughout the years. At work, I was balanced, poised, and professional. I would walk in with a smile on my face, go to my office, shut the door, and act out with Internet pornography and chat rooms. When I was with my college friends, I was the baby. I played the "innocent" codependent Marnie, the "good girl," the Marnie who never drank, but just took care of the rest of the bunch when they did. At church I was the devout Christian, pseudo listening from the concrete bench outside, but making sure my friends and family all knew I was present and accounted for. But the real Marnie, the uninhibited Marnie, surfaced after work hours where I would spend most of my free time at bars with the "good old boys club." I could tell a good dirty joke or two and just be one of the guys. The more I drank, the more I talked. The more I talked, the more I started blaming my circumstances for my behavior. My drinking buddies got the unvarnished story of how awful life was like for me at home. I became completely cavalier with a complete disregard and disrespect for myself and for those around me. My life was a riotous mess.

My insatiable appetite for more manifested itself as I attempted to fill the void within me, only to find out that this beast of ugliness would, in no way, be satisfied. My form of self-punishment and control was to starve my body, both spiritually and physically. Body image became more important to me than anything else in my life, including the people I loved the most. I was now on a quest for the perfect figure, no matter what the cost. Starving myself made me feel like I was making my own decisions. I put myself on a rigid diet which consisted of a handful of grapes each day and excessive amounts of Diet Coke. I decided what I put in my body. I decided what I would look like. I started working out obsessively, running between twelve and fifteen miles a day. This lifestyle, coupled with my sexual addiction, left my body weak and out of fuel. I weighed a mere ninety-two pounds, with a sunken face, and was rapidly self-destructing. My addiction was now in full throttle.

As I saw the scenes of my life unfolding, I became desperate to find freedom from my "web of deception." I picked up the phone and called Saddleback Church and they suggested I try Celebrate Recovery. During that time, I recalled the Christian values taught to me as a child by my grandparents, which I had buried due to my anger and resentment toward God. He had finally gotten my attention. It was then that I realized, *"I don't understand myself at all, for I really want to do what is right, but I can't. I do what I don't want to—what I hate. I know perfectly well that what I am doing is wrong, and my bad conscience proves that I agree with these laws I am breaking. But I can't help myself, because I'm no longer doing it. It is sin inside me that is stronger than I am that makes me do these evil things"* (Romans 7:15–20). At this point, I felt as if I had been hollowed out and the world, as I knew it, was slowly being erased. I didn't know how to reconcile these conflicting pieces of my past. The pain had finally become greater than the fear. I had reached my bottom.

Two months after that first fateful night at Celebrate Recovery, a women's step study group opened. So I picked up a Celebrate Recovery Bible and a set of Celebrate Recovery participant's guides and began a pilgrimage through the Christ-centered 12 Steps with women I could relate to and who could also relate to me . . . and where secrets seemed all but impossible. At first I kept myself at a safe distance. I would guard my secrets so that no one could use what they knew to hurt me. I also felt hideously ugly, and thought the scars that had been left behind were visible to everyone. But, as I began to share, for the first time I saw women who just stayed silent throughout, listening without judgment. I began to grasp that this internal battle I was having was not uncommon. It was then that I started to understand how the pains of my past played a crucial part in my behavior. I started realizing that I was in a cycle of addiction. All my life I viewed men as objects, and I was imitating what I had learned in my childhood. I had kept *so* many secrets — childhood secrets, secrets in my adult life, and secrets in my marriage — but by saying them out loud, it brought some truth to my reality. I found comfort in the fact that I could not be perfect — there was no such thing as the perfect marriage or the perfect body. Most importantly, I saw just how far I had fallen away from my relationship with Christ. *"Problems far too big for me to solve are piled higher than my head. Meanwhile my sins too many to count; have all caught up with me and I am ashamed to look up" (Psalm 40:12).*

Principle 4 says, "Openly examine and confess my faults to myself, to God, and to someone I trust." "Happy are the pure in heart" (Matthew 5:8).

I began exploring this new, unchartered territory at Celebrate Recovery by working this principle, and the true healing began. It was then I heard God's promise of freedom and stopped acting out. *"It was then that I realized that whatever is covered up will be uncovered, and every secret will be made known. So then, whatever you have said in the dark will be heard in broad daylight"* (Luke 12:2–3).

As I laid my sins at the foot of the cross and turned from my addictions, God declared me not guilty. *He "blotted out the charges proved against you, the list of his commandments which you had not obeyed. He took this list of sins and destroyed it by nailing it to Christ's cross"* (Colossians 2:13–15).

I have reconciled my relationship with my husband and today my relationships are built on honesty and trust. My marriage has been restored. The challenges are still there. Marriage takes work. And my view on marriage is that every couple needs to argue every now and then, just to prove that the relationship is strong enough to survive it. We have been blessed with the most precious gifts of all, two beautiful baby girls. My new ministry in life is my family. Where they once played second fiddle to my work and my addictive behavior, they are now my priority. In fact, in this day and age, where people are so accessible with smart phones, iPads, iPods, etc., our family has a rule: "No electronics at the table." Most importantly, I am teaching my children that NOTHING is more important than my time with them. No email, text, tweet, phone call, whatever.

As for my mom and dad, I have found it in my heart to forgive them, although I still do not have a relationship with either of them. Though I have made attempts over the years, I remain steadfast in the fact that neither of them are safe people to have around me, my husband, or my girls. Neither of them has changed their behaviors, and unfortunately, they have been left to live in their own misery. I have learned how to embrace my pain and made the choice to abandon my life of deception and destruction.

As I reflect on my life now, I thank God for His never-failing truth and understanding. I look back at the journey I had to take through Celebrate Recovery to bring balance to the chaos of my life, and now the blessings that come with being able to help people use Celebrate Recovery as a tool to implement peace and joy in their own lives. I have used these same tools to continue my obedience and submission to Christ as a wife, mother, and employee. God has taken my tragedy and used it as a testament of my faith. Most of all, I thank God that, unlike Delilah, mine is not "a life wasted," and that He chose to spare me rather than erase me from history as He did Delilah. I'm no longer defined by my past mistakes and failures. It's only by God's grace that today, when I look at myself in the mirror, I no longer see myself as someone trying to be perfect, or an adulterer, or an alcoholic, or anorexic. I see myself as an incredibly blessed mother, wife, and forgiven child of God.

In corporate America I used to fly every week and find myself in compromising situations because of my husband's absence. Ironically, God is using the very same pattern of flying that was so instrumental in virtually destroying my life to restore me to wholeness. Today I get to serve on the Celebrate Recovery conference team, where it is my privilege to travel every other week to different cities nationally and internationally to help coordinate Celebrate Recovery one-day seminars. My accountability team now spans the nation, as I have filled my life with godly women and men from whom I seek guidance every day. With an accountability partner in almost every state, there's no hiding anymore.

This reminds me of God's promise that says, *"Even though you are at the ends of the earth, the LORD your God will go and find you and bring you back again"* (Deuteronomy 30:4).

You know, *"there was a time when I wouldn't admit what a sinner I was. But my dishonesty made me miserable and filled my days with frustration. All day and all night your hand was heavy on me. My strength evaporated like water on a sunny day until I finally admitted all my sins to you and stopped trying to hide them. I said to myself, 'I will confess them to the LORD.' And you forgave me! All my guilt is gone"* (Psalm 32:3–5).

Thank you for letting me share.

Principle 5

> **Principle 5:** Voluntarily submit to every change God wants to make in my life and humbly ask Him to remove my character defects.
>
> *"Happy are those whose greatest desire is to do what God requires."*
> *(Matthew 5:6)*

By the time you get to Principle 5, you will have already taken some major steps on the road to recovery. You admitted you had a problem that you were powerless within yourself to overcome. You came to believe that God could and would help you. You have sought Him and turned your life and will over to His care and direction. You've taken a spiritual inventory and shared it both with God and with another person. That was a lot of work—hard work, great work! Now you will be asking God to remove your character defects.

Principle 5 states that each of us is ready to voluntarily submit to every change God wants to make in our lives. The sixth and seventh steps of the Christ-centered 12 Steps relate to Principle 5.

> **Step 6:** We were entirely ready to have God remove all these defects of character.
>
> *"Humble yourselves before the Lord, and he will lift you up."*
> *(James 4:10)*

> **Step 7:** We humbly asked Him to remove all our shortcomings.
>
> *"If we confess our sins, he is faithful and just and will forgive us our sins and purify us from all unrighteousness." (1 John 1:9)*

Most, if not all, of us would be more than willing to have *certain* character defects go away. The sooner the better, we think. Good riddance! But the truth is that some defects are hard to give up. Like weeds in a garden, they've developed deep roots. We've developed our defects of character, our hang-ups, and our destructive habits over periods of five, ten, twenty or more years. In this principle you and God—together—are going after these defects. *All* of them.

To make these positive changes in our lives, we need to be entirely ready to let God be our life-changer. We're not the how-and-when committee. We're the preparation committee. All we have to be is ready.

Sometimes we discover in ourselves so many character defects that it's hard to know where to start. We need to go back to the wrongs, shortcomings, and sins we identified in our Principle 4 inventories. Remember, falling down doesn't make us a failure; staying down does. God doesn't just want us to admit our wrongs; He wants to make us right. He wants to give us "hope and a future" (Jeremiah 29:11). God doesn't just want to forgive us; He wants to change us. We need to ask Him first to remove those character defects that are causing us the most pain. Ask Him today, and be specific.

At first, our old self-doubts and low self-image may tell us we're not worthy of the growth and progress we're already making in the program. We need to turn off those old, negative tapes and yield to the growth. It's the Holy Spirit's work within us. Through His transforming power, we'll find the victory that keeps us from reverting back to our hang-ups and harmful habits.

Once we ask God to remove our character defects, we begin a journey that will lead us to new freedom from our past. We need to be careful not to look for perfection but instead to rejoice in steady progress. We need to seek, and be satisfied with, steady improvement.

The victory we receive in Principle 5 is summed up in Romans 12:2: "Do not conform to the pattern of this world, but be transformed by the renewing of your mind. Then you will be able to test and approve what God's will is—his good, pleasing and perfect will."

Principle 5 Prayer

Dear God, thank You for taking me this far on my recovery journey. Now I pray for Your help in making me entirely ready to change my destructive patterns. Give me the strength to deal with the character defects I've turned over to You. Allow me to accept all the changes You want to make in me. Help me to be the person You want me to be. In Your Son's name I pray, Amen.

PRINCIPLE 5 TESTIMONY

My name is John, and I am a grateful believer in Jesus Christ who struggles with codependency.

My earliest memories are probably kindergarten and the beginning of grade school. I was a pretty happy and extroverted little fella. I was very active, full of joy and energy, secure and comfortable in my own skin. We were Mom, Dad, my older brother (by three years), and then twin sisters a year younger—all together in Duluth, Minnesota. My parents were saved and belonged to an exciting new independent Pentecostal church. They were young and zealous, and had young and zealous friends, and a young and zealous pastor. My father worked at a men's clothing store and my mom stayed home with us kids. Some of the families from our young and zealous church got together and decided to buy some property just outside the city limits in a lovely, private wooded area. They all wanted to build some homes together, form a Christian neighborhood, with Christian kids riding their Christian bikes on a Christian road, with Christian dogs chasing Christian cats ...

Our family quickly signed on to that project and soon we were living in a freshly built log home on Morning Star Drive.

I guess I was in the second grade or so when, one by one, each of us four clueless siblings was called upstairs into our parents' bedroom for news of the divorce. This is how Mom wanted to break it to us. This is one of my few branded-in memories. I remember the unfinished texture of the wooden baluster on the balcony, my hand sort of trailing behind me on the railing trying to somehow slow my progress to my father and mother's room. My older brother came out sobbing, and I just kept walking toward their room, straining to look through their cracked door. There was something evil crouched beyond that door: depression, pain ... unwelcome, unasked-for change.

It was so quiet after the divorce announcement. My parents used to fight a lot before the announcement, but now my dad hadn't the spirit for fighting; he gave up. Again, the realization of past yelling matches came *after* the hush fell on that big log home. My father, one of the heroes, if there are any in this testimony, was so infinitely sad. My mom knew the pain she was causing—I do believe that—but at the same time, I have come to understand that she didn't. She was not making decisions based on the truth. She was lying to herself, and to us, about how much fun her new life, *our* new life, would be. It was a fresh start, a new and exciting adventure. Her world was a cleverly constructed fantasy of greener grass.

She packed us up and moved us away from my father, to a farm where a new family was waiting. I remember her turning her head to us in the passenger and back seats while driving and repeating over and over, "Isn't this exciting?"

At the first meeting of the soon-to-be-step-family, I remember lots of dogs and the smell of a dairy farm. I was game; it DID look exciting. My sisters took things in stride as well, but my older brother did not. I *adapted* to this new life. I did whatever I was told; I was compliant; I had fun; I rode motorcycles; I pitched in with the haying; I picked rocks in the fields; I camped out with my stepbrother; I shot a pistol, rode the three-wheeler, grabbed an electric fence on a dare to see who could hold on the longest. I did it. I conformed. My brother did not.

In the midst of my mother's chaotic relationship with this new husband, my brother went a little crazy. Our oldest stepbrother was a bullying beast of a teenager who had his father's temper. He was full of hate, full of rage, and I stayed out of his way, laughed at his dirty jokes, did what I was told. My brother did not laugh, did not do what he was told, did not stay out of anyone's way.

One night, out in the barn, my older brother had enough of our "bully stepbrother" and tried to crush his head with a lead pipe. He whiffed badly. I watched as my brother paid a terrible price for standing up to a bully. It was a terrifying experience, which led to me and my brother both moving back to our dad's. My brother and I carried on a new existence at my father's home in that huge, empty log tomb. Dad was not coping well, and we weren't enough to keep him going. He had seen his church collapse a few months earlier in a scandal. His church, his marriage, and his life had been taken from him; the rug had been pulled out; that was his new reality and ours.

Somewhere in the transition from grade school to middle school, depression took me like anesthesia. I remember it coming on, then I remember coming out of it. I ate a lot, I know that. I was like a Hoover vacuum on a very low setting. Whatever food was near me got sucked in, slowly but surely. I stared at whatever TV had to offer for hours after school, when other kids were outside playing. I began to skip school, constantly faking migraines. My mother was divorced again and off the farm. *I didn't care, I was depressed.* She had repented of her foolishness, and my brother and I were going to live with her and my sisters again in a nice little duplex. *I didn't care, I was depressed.* I was back with mom, my sisters, and my brother, and I was put in counseling. Now, I did care about that. I hated that. Maybe my hating counseling shocked me out of my depression. Counseling scared me straight.

When I did awaken from my depressed stupor, I found myself in the body of this scared, fat, introverted older kid. Mom was on welfare trying to get an education so I wore a lot of secondhand clothing. Bullies were a terror to me. I was much larger than most kids my age, but I was afraid of everyone. I was what others said I was. There was no doubt in my mind. I just wanted to disappear.

That's how I coped. I began to deal with problems through invisibility. A very big boy willing every part of his being to disappear into thin air best describes me at this time of my life. I was living a life of "quiet desperation." I was tortured and tormented by my classmates, physically and emotionally abused, and I felt like I deserved it.

I was helpless, powerless, and daily frozen with fear, being constantly silenced by crippling insecurity. This overwhelming insecurity at times reclaims its hold on me. A strange residual social fear lingers, but I have learned to trust that it remains for God's purposes. I choose to embrace this weakness and say with Paul: *"His power is perfected in my weakness. When I am weak, I am truly strong."*

One day it all began to change. It started when I stood up to a guy in my class who wanted to take my seat, and what do you know, he backed down. I started lifting weights, then I went by myself and tried out for the football team, and I made it. Then I went to the church youth group, started cracking jokes, starting talking to girls. By my junior year of high school, I was starting for the varsity football team and ENJOYING school for the first time in my life.

My grades stunk, but I was happy and independent. I had been getting more and more involved in the youth group, and I began developing a vibrant relationship with God. I had prayed for salvation at five years of age with my father, but now I was beginning to understand and answer a clear call to His service. At fifteen, I seriously committed myself to Jesus Christ. I made a vow to live for Him for the rest of my life.

I graduated from high school and eventually moved with my mom to the Twin Cities where I was back to being a "nobody." I had been lightly recruited by a couple local colleges for football and had received a small scholarship at a Christian university in Missouri, but that insecurity came back stronger than ever, convincing me all efforts to succeed were hopeless. I began a slow and steady roll back into depression. I was not in church, not in school. I was back to a day-to-day existence without meaning, without purpose, working the graveyard shift at a local gas station. My mom had many relationships over the years following the farm with one deadbeat after the other; but in St. Paul, Minnesota, she picked up their king in a bar one summer evening.

He told her that he was the son of a wealthy CEO, and that he would pay her back if she would spring for a weekend of partying in Duluth. He had no intention of paying for anything; he wasn't the son of a CEO; he was a con man running up her credit cards, depleting her savings, until finally he showed his true colors. One evening he took the rented Cadillac my mother had charged for their lavish weekend fantasy and disappeared. After my mom called the police a few days after his departure, I found him late one night passed out on the seat of the stolen Caddy.

I wanted to save my mom from these guys every time. She was always able to sell me on them, and then when she turned against them, I was right there with her, comforting her, consoling. I was blinded to her responsibility in these situations. I wanted to be somebody's favorite — to save someone — and she was beginning to rely on my shoulder to cry on. No matter what she had done to me, or to the family over the years, I loved her, I still believed in her, she relied on me, and that was what I desperately clung to. So, I called the police on the loser in the Caddy, and I was the hero, until my mom decided to bail the con man out of jail. When she walked through the door with him, I almost fell out of my chair. The king was back. I gave my mom an ultimatum. I was amazed and hysterical with anger when she gave me her answer. No. This man would stay, and I would go. Back to my dad's I went.

Soon after moving back to my father's, I had an opportunity to move north and play football at a community college. It was at this remote, "nowhere" school that I learned about the wonderful numbing effects of alcohol. It was easy to let it all go there in Virginia, Minnesota. I was alone, I was depressed, and I was a waste. My life consisted of football, a meager schedule of classes, alcohol whenever and however I could get it, and a girlfriend hand-picked to put up with my moodiness and drinking. I had plugged into a local church the moment I arrived, but it couldn't hold me; I was just too wrapped up in my pain, in coping. The discovery of alcohol was a revelation. It made me more depressed, but in a bittersweet, self-pitying, brooding sense.

I dropped out of college after my first year, and ended up rooming with my best friend from high school back in Duluth. I began working another graveyard shift cleaning the floors at a grocery store. I was sleeping through the days, stockpiling alcohol on the shelf, working a dead-end job that I could barely hold, picking fights. Now *I* was becoming the bully. I would drink at home, and then go out drinking, drive home drunk, and drink. There was nothing else in my future. This was my life, for the rest of my life.

One night I was alone, and I was sober, or I was drunk, or someplace in between. I do remember the shotgun in my hands. I had my grandfather's double barreled shotgun across my lap. I tried to put it to my head, but fear swept over me. Was I so pathetic that I couldn't even kill myself?

I began playing games with loading it and trying to peek down the barrel to see if I could get up the courage to take this seriously. I wept and screamed on the floor of my room for God to save me, but I was alone. He must have had enough and abandoned me; I couldn't blame Him. I wanted Him to leave me alone; I didn't deserve love. I was going to die, and I was going to be as insignificant in death as I was in life.

I was finally ready. Calm and determined, sniffing away the last of the tears, I said my last half-hearted prayer, "Lord, if You're there, it's time to let me know, or I'm finished." Another ridiculous ultimatum.

But, in that little upstairs apartment, God answered me. The room glossed over, and I was in a cave. Ribs became part of the infrastructure of the room, and I was inside something. It was a vision. The only one I have ever had. And it wasn't angels and harps. It was me clearly in the inner guts of a fish. I grabbed hold of that vision with two desperate hands, finding and opening my old Bible from youth group. I had no idea where the story of Jonah was. It was a book in itself. The story was familiar, but what did that have to do with me? Then I saw it, the prayer in the second chapter. Jonah's prayer is what was in me. My spirit had been speaking this in groans, in the throes of anguish. *"In my distress I called to the LORD, and he answered me. From the depths of the grave I called for help, and you listened to me cry ... I said, 'I have been banished from your sight' ... The engulfing waters threatened me, the deep surrounded me ... To the roots of the mountains I sank down; the earth beneath barred me in forever. But you brought my life up from the pit, O LORD my God. When my life was ebbing away, I remembered you, LORD, and my prayer rose to you ... What I have vowed I will make good. I will say, 'Salvation comes from the LORD'"* (Jonah 2:1–9).

I dedicated myself to the Lord that moment, telling Him that what I had vowed as a committed Christian in my youth, I would make good.

I signed up for the fall to go to the Christian university in Missouri where I had initially, upon graduation, received a seed scholarship for football. I had no idea where the funds would come from, but it was clear that was the place God wanted me. It was where He had wanted me all along. I had been running from a call. Like Jonah.

I was accepted to the school and the money somehow was there for me to attend. Life was so sweet these three years of school. I was away at school, playing football. I had Christ-centered classes and Christian friends, so why was I still struggling to maintain my sobriety? There were rules against drinking. I had even signed a covenant that I would abstain from alcohol. But that didn't mean opportunities didn't present themselves; it didn't mean opportunities weren't created. My last binge ended late one night after staring into the disappointed eyes of the most beautiful woman God has ever breathed life into. My girlfriend had been able to melt away some of the walls that were again forming around me—we even began talking about marriage, about kids, about everything—but we hadn't talked about this drinking stuff before.

Another stamped-in, burned-in memory is when I stopped by her off-campus apartment after having a few drinks, and then a few more drinks with some friends who lived in the same apartment complex. My girlfriend didn't say so, but it was all over her face when she saw me. She was disappointed. I don't think she ever really thought twice about us—we were in love and flying recklessly and blissfully toward our future—but in that instant, I saw a loss of respect ... even some doubt. She loved me for the right reasons—for the Christian man I wanted to be—and this wasn't it. It was in this moment, confronted with this past-and-once-again-present coping strategy, that the double-standard I was keeping between my Christian ascent and my worldly descent came to a head. I was either going to become the man God had created and called *or* go back to despair, loneliness, death, and hell. I chose life, and have never, in over a decade of sobriety, ever regretted my decision.

My girlfriend and I got married, and I received a degree in criminal justice, but ended up enjoying a counseling group I was placed in during my practicum so much that I began to explore counseling and social work as a career. Together we moved to my wife's home state of Delaware where I began working for the state's Division of Family Services as a family crisis therapist.

During my five years in that office, I toiled through a master's program in social work, and began group and individual work at a private counseling agency on the side to earn hours for my clinical licensing. I loved the work, I loved counseling, and I loved group process.

What I didn't realize is that in working two to three jobs ministering to others, I was neglecting my ministry at home to my family. Three jobs at times kept me away constantly, and I was even volunteering any leftover hours at the church. It was exhausting—and a trying time for my marriage.

I tried to convince my wife, unsuccessfully, that this work was my mission field. I was giving my all in answer to "the call." But my absence was wearing on her, on us. We had two girls, and I didn't see much of them. My explanation to them, to myself, and to God was that I was needed out there; people needed me; they needed saving! She had her parents to lean on, my kids had their grandparents. Those I helped didn't have anyone but me. Isn't being a Christian about helping the helpless AT ANY COST?

What I didn't fully realize is that through college, working toward a degree, playing football, and now with my career goals, my master's degree, my striving for success in counseling others, I was succumbing to the pressure of trying to earn back my value. The value I had lost by being a fat, spineless nobody without any answers. My professional life was a tenuous balance of keeping everyone happy with me, spinning anything negative, running from conflict, blaming others, justifying my very existence, running, running to keep that distance ... keeping the helpless loser I once was far behind me.

One day, God called me to a fast. A one-week fast. I managed to doubt it and fight it for a good month, but I finally relented. When the fast was over, I was incredibly disappointed. No lightning bolts, no giant handwriting on the wall.

What a rip-off! Oh well. It was done and I had been obedient. A few weeks later, my brother-in-law, a youth pastor working in a little church in West Virginia, called and asked if I would travel to West Virginia to talk to his church's men's ministry about outreach.

His pastor had felt God leading the church to do more for those outside their four walls. I said I would be glad to do it, and soon found myself talking to a small group of men in Clarksburg, West Virginia about Celebrate Recovery, and some other outreach programs I was heading up in our church in Delaware.

A week later, I was being asked to consider interviewing in this same church to do outreach ministry full-time. God was orchestrating a miraculous life-change, and soon I was chugging through the mountains in a U-Haul contemplating this new direction in my life and ministry.

Now the recovery program I had started in Delaware was very loosely based on the Celebrate Recovery curriculum, and I had plans in West Virginia to veer even further off the Celebrate Recovery course. I have since discovered why I was reluctant to conform to the program. Running my own program, my way, was all about pride. Tailor-making my own recovery program elevated me to the keeper of all the keys, giving me the illusion of being in complete control and helping me stay aloof in a "therapist" role. It kept people looking to me for the answers. I wanted to be their savior. *"I, even I, am the LORD, and apart from me there is no savior" (Isaiah 43:11).*

After several months of running the "John" recovery program in my new ministerial role in West Virginia, with frustratingly minimal success, my wonderful little church sent me to my first Celebrate Recovery Summit. It was during those three days in August 2006 where I felt challenged to make a commitment to run this ministry by the letter. I had been fighting it, as I was to learn later, mainly because I would rather help "those people," than be *one* of "those people."

However, as I listened to the testimonies given at the Summit, as I worshiped with the thousands of lives being transformed by the power of God through the truths of this program, I felt the gentle conviction of the Holy Spirit calling me to submit and SURRENDER. I had been asking everyone to share their lives with me, to open up, be completely transparent so they could find healing and hope for their lives. However, I had never really done that myself. What hypocrisy! During a question-and-answer time at one of the Summit workshops, I made a public confession that I had been using the Celebrate Recovery name, but had not been following the model. It was at that vulnerable place, the giving up of my power, where my own healing began. You could say that my journey of discovery into my own emotional and spiritual DNA finally began when I submitted to the Celebrate Recovery DNA.

While I had been trying to construct a new me through meeting the needs of others, God had wanted nothing more than to deconstruct me by exposing my own many hurts, hang-ups, and habits. Through the work of this ministry, especially going through the step study, I finally dared to get honest about my past.

Principle 5 says, "Voluntarily submit to every change God wants to make in my life and humbly ask Him to remove my character defects." "Happy are those whose greatest desire is to do what God requires" (Matthew 5:6).

Finally, I would have to take a real look at myself and either change or continue in my own pride and ego. Then, as I wrote my inventory, I realized something that broke me to a point where I hadn't been broken before. I started to see and feel how much my efforts to replace God with self-sufficiency and self-righteousness had grieved my God and Savior Jesus Christ. After sharing my inventory, with the help of another minister, I made my first heart-wrenching amends. My first amends were offered to God, and through that process I felt His forgiveness, mercy, and love for me like never before.

In that place of grace, He gave me a new awareness of a value I could never earn, and a value I will never lose.

"How deep the Father's love for us, how vast beyond all measure that He would send His only Son, to make a wretch His treasure."

Today I have come to a new realization and reliance on His economy. It is not by my strength, not by man's might, but truly by His Spirit that I (and others) find true recovery. My wife and I celebrated our twelfth anniversary in June. I have four beautiful daughters. (Yes, I am powerless and my life is truly unmanageable.) My family has now become my most important and cherished ministry.

I want to encourage anyone who is feeling the overwhelming weight of insecurity to let go, get vulnerable, and trust in the Lord. In Principle 7 we are taught: "Reserve a daily time with God for self-examination, Bible reading, and prayer in order to know God and His will for my life and to gain the power to follow His *will."* Celebrate Recovery rightly emphasizes this complete dependency on Christ as the only opportunity we have for true peace, security, and salvation.

I thank God for His love, and I thank God for my family; I thank God for this program and for my incredible Celebrate Recovery family; and I thank God for the opportunity to share my testimony with you.

Thank you for letting me share.

Principle 6

> **Principle 6:** Evaluate all my relationships. Offer forgiveness to those who have hurt me and make amends for harm I've done to others, except when to do so would harm them or others.
>
> *"Happy are the merciful."* (Matthew 5:7)
>
> *"Happy are the peacemakers."* (Matthew 5:9)

Principle 6 is all about making amends and offering forgiveness. "Forgive me as I learn to forgive" sums up Principle 6. This is right in line with Jesus' words in the prayer He taught his disciples: "Forgive us our debts, as we also have forgiven our debtors" (Matthew 6:12). But some of us balk at making amends. If God has forgiven me, we think, isn't that enough? Why should I dredge up the past? After all, making amends doesn't sound natural. The answer to that objection is simple: Making amends isn't about our past so much as it is about our future. Before we can enjoy the healthy relationships we desire, we need to clean out the guilt, shame, and pain that have caused many of our past relationships to fail.

Luke 6:31 instructs each of us to "do to others as you would have them do to you." This verse reminds us to treat others the way we want to be treated. For some of us, that may be difficult. We've been badly hurt and/or abused. Many of us had nothing to do with the wrongs committed against us.

The first part of Principle 6, "Evaluate all my relationships," deals with our willingness to consider making amends and offering our forgiveness. The second part, "Offer forgiveness to those who have hurt me and make amends for harm I've done to others," calls us to action. We need to pull out the dead weeds in our past broken relationships so that we can clear a place where new relationships can be successfully planted or old ones nurtured. That's why this principle is so important.

It's so important to make amends because we can become addicted to our bitterness, hatred, and revenge, just as we may have become addicted to alcohol, drugs, or unhealthy relationships. A life characterized by bitterness, resentment, and anger will kill us emotionally and shrivel our souls. Such a life will produce the three Ds:

Depression
Despair
Discouragement

An unforgiving heart will cause us more pain and destruction than it will ever cause the person who has hurt us.

The inability to accept and offer forgiveness can stall, block, or even destroy our recovery. Forgiveness breaks that negative cycle. It doesn't settle all the questions of blame, justice, or fairness, but it does allow relationships to heal.

Principle 6 addresses three types of forgiveness. The first and most important kind of forgiveness is extended by God to us. Have we accepted God's forgiveness? Have we accepted Jesus' work on the cross? By His willingness to take our punishment, all our sins were canceled. Our debt was paid in full—a free gift for those who are willing to put their faith in Him as the true and only Higher Power, Savior, and Lord. Jesus Himself exclaimed from the cross, "It is finished" (John 19:30)—possibly the most significant three words ever uttered. No matter how grievously we may have injured others or ourselves, the grace of God is always sufficient. His forgiveness is always complete, with no strings attached.

The second kind of forgiveness is the kind we extend from ourselves to others. This type of forgiveness is a process. We first need to be willing to forgive. But in order to become truly free, we have to let go of the pain of the past harm and abuse caused by others.

The third kind of forgiveness may well be the most difficult for us to extend: We need to forgive ourselves. We may find the grace within ourselves to forgive others, and we may accept God's forgiveness, but we may feel as though the guilt and shame of our own past are just too horrendous to forgive. But this is what God wants to do with the darkness of our past: "'Come now, let us settle the matter,' says the Lord. 'Though your sins are like scarlet, they shall be as white as snow; though they are red as crimson, they shall be like wool'" (Isaiah 1:18). No matter how unloved or worthless we may feel, God loves us and values us highly. Our feelings about ourselves don't change God's assessment of us and our potential one bit.

As we grow as Christians and move through our recovery process, we want to follow the guidance and direction of Jesus Christ. As we get to know Him better, we want to model His teachings and His ways. We want to become more like Him. If we're going to implement Principle 6 to the best of our ability, we need to learn to model God's grace.

As we learn to model God's grace, we'll be able to complete Principle 6 and discover healing in our lost and broken relationships—at least as far as that healing depends upon our action. As Romans 12:18 directs us: "If it is possible, as far as it depends on you, live at peace with everyone."

The eighth and ninth steps of the Christ-centered 12 Steps relate to Principle 6.

Step 8: We made a list of all persons we had harmed and became willing to make amends to them all.

"Do to others as you would have them do to you." (Luke 6:31)

Step 9: We made direct amends to such people whenever possible, except when to do so would injure them or others.

"Therefore, if you are offering your gift at the altar and there remember that your brother or sister has something against you, leave your gift there in front of the altar. First go and be reconciled to them; then come and offer your gift." (Matthew 5:23–24)

Forgiveness is all about letting go. Remember playing tug-of-war as a child? As long as the people on each end of the rope are tugging, you have a war. You let go of your end of the rope when you forgive others. No matter how hard they may tug on their end, if you've released yours, the war is over. But until you release that rope, you're a prisoner of war.

Principle 6 Prayer

Dear God, thank You for Your love, for the grace You freely offer. Help me model Your ways when I make my amends to those I've hurt and offer my forgiveness to those who've injured me. Help me set aside my selfishness and speak the truth in love. Help me focus on my own responsibility in the issue, so my actions won't be conditional. I know I can forgive others because You first forgave me. Thank You for loving me. In Jesus' name I pray, Amen.

Principle 7

Principle 7: Reserve a daily time with God for self-examination, Bible reading, and prayer in order to know God and His will for my life and to gain the power to follow His will.

"Happy are the pure in heart." (Matthew 5:8)

When you get to Principle 7, you will have arrived at an important junction. You will have come to understand that you could never have made it this far on your own power. In fact, the only reason you were able to have reached this point is the decision you made way back in Principle 3 to turn over your life and will to God's care.

Jesus explains it this way in John 8:31–32: "If you hold to my teaching, you are really my disciples. Then you will know the truth, and the truth will set you free." Then in John 14:6 He defines truth by identifying it with Himself: "I am the way and the truth and the life. No one comes to the Father except through me." We've been set free from our habits because of the Truth (Jesus Christ) we've invited into our hearts.

Step 10: We continued to take personal inventory and, when we were wrong, promptly admitted it.

"So, if you think you are standing firm, be careful that you don't fall!" (1 Corinthians 10:12)

We've arrived at the crossroads of our recoveries. This isn't a place to stop and rest on our past accomplishments. We need to thank God for getting us this far on our road to recovery; to praise Him for the many victories over our hurts, hang-ups, and habits that we've already seen in working the first six principles; and to continue working the last two principles with the same devotion and enthusiasm that got us to this point in our recoveries. First Corinthians 10:12 puts it this way: "If you think you are standing firm, be careful that you don't fall!"

Most recovery material refers to Steps 10 through 12 (Principles 7 and 8) as the maintenance steps. It's certainly true that in these principles we'll live out our recoveries for the remainder of our time here on earth—one day at a time! But we need to do much more than just maintain our recoveries; we need to continue to *grow* them.

In Principle 7 we desire to grow daily in our new relationships with Jesus Christ and others. Instead of attempting to be in control of every situation and every person with whom we come into contact, or instead of spinning out of control ourselves, we're starting to exhibit self-control, living the way God wants us to. Remember that "self under control" is what we're initially seeking but that self under *God's* control is what we're ultimately striving for.

As we begin to work Principle 7 and Step 10, we'll see that this step involves three key actions:

1. Taking time to do a daily inventory.
2. Evaluating both the good and the bad.
3. Admitting our wrongs promptly.

One way to keep daily track of our good and bad behaviors is to keep a journal. Our journal isn't a place to jot down the calories we ingested for lunch today or our carpool schedule for school. It's a tool for us to review and record the good and bad things we did today. We can look for negative patterns, issues that we're repeatedly writing down and having to make amends for. We can share these pitfalls with our sponsors or accountability partners and set up an action plan to overcome them with God's help.

Journaling will help us live in daily humility — in reality, not in denial. Through God's guidance we can make choices about the emotions that affect our thinking and actions. When we take this step seriously, we can begin to take positive action — instead of getting caught up in a continuous spiral of *reaction*.

In Principle 7, we actually do three different inventories:

1. *An ongoing inventory.* We can maintain an ongoing inventory throughout the day. The best time to admit we're wrong is at the exact time we're made aware of it. Why wait?

2. *A daily inventory.* At the end of each day we can look back over our daily activities, both the good and the bad, paying special attention to points at which we might have harmed someone else or reacted out of anger or fear. But once again, we need to remember to keep our daily inventory balanced. We should be sure to include the things we did right throughout the day, no matter how easy they may be to overlook or discount.

3. *A periodic inventory.* We should take a periodic inventory every ninety days or so. We may want to get away on a mini retreat. We should bring our daily journal with us, and pray as we read through the entries for the last ninety days. We should ask God to show us areas in our life in which we can improve during the next ninety days. But we should also remember to identify and celebrate the victories we've already experienced.

Principle 7 is so important. It also includes Step 11 of the Christ-centered 12 Steps.

Step 11: We sought through prayer and meditation to improve our conscious contact with God, praying only for knowledge of His will for us and power to carry that out.

"Let the word of Christ dwell in you richly." (Colossians 3:16)

By this point in our recoveries we've learned that when we start our day working Principle 7 and having a quiet time with God, and when we end it by doing our daily inventory, we have a pretty good day—a reasonably happy day. Not only will this help to prevent relapse, but it will cultivate in us an attitude of gratitude.

To help maintain this grateful attitude, we can focus our thankfulness on at least four areas of our lives: God, others, our recovery, and our church.

Principle 7 Prayer

Dear God, help me to set aside the hassles and racket of the world, so I can focus my mind and listen just to You for the next few minutes. Help me to get to know You better. Help me to better understand Your plan and purpose for my life. Father, help me to live this day within the boundaries of today, seeking Your will and living this one day as You would have me live it.

I pray that others may view me as Yours, not just in my words but, more importantly, in my actions. Thank You for Your love, Your grace, Your perfect forgiveness. Thank You for all those important individuals You've placed in my life—in my program, in my recovery, and within my church family. Your will be done, not mine. In Your Son's name I pray, Amen.

PRINCIPLE 7 TESTIMONY

My name is Monty, I am a grateful believer in Jesus Christ who struggles with gambling.

I was born in a little town called Okemah, Oklahoma. My dad met my mom after he returned from World War II; he was in the Army, where he drove tanks. My mom, on the other hand, was one of seven siblings raised on a farm not far from Okemah. I came into this world at about one o'clock in the morning January 2, 1951, and just nine months later we were living in Richmond, California, across the bay from San Francisco.

I entered into the first grade in Richmond, but my dad had so many different jobs, we moved so many times, and I attended so many schools that I didn't stay long enough to pass the first grade. That's right, I flunked the first grade. I remember feeling very stupid and not like other kids who had no problem passing the easiest grade in school. This affected my educational outlook for most of my first twelve school years. My grades were barely passing all the way until I graduated from high school. But I got my diploma!

At my graduation, when they were calling out each of the names of my classmates to receive their rolled-up reward for twelve long years of both good teachers and bad, it was my turn to be handed my diploma. Over the loud speaker came someone else's name, not mine.

I know my face must have shown an expression of failure because at that moment I went back in time to being a five-year old again. I was being told by a loudspeaker—to all my friends, family, and everyone in the bleachers—"YOU FLUNKED."

I was dumbfounded and embarrassed, but the wise teacher who was giving out the diplomas held my right hand in a very tight adult handshake, looked at me and my horrified expression, and then whispered in a calm voice, "Just wait!"

The next name, read loud and clear, was mine. Wow, close call! But I made it, and now it was time for the next step in my education: "finally" off to college in the fall.

In college, I had professors and instructors teaching everything from math, science, and logic to history, English, and world religions including Christianity, Hinduism, Islam, Buddhism, and Atheism. I met students who claimed to be witches and followers of Scientology, Mormonism, Jehovah's Witness, and other cults. Of course, I had my own brand of homemade religion that I believed which I called Monty-theism.

This religion was made up in my own mind, not from any Bible or any formal religion, just my own way of believing. But it was this very belief system that formed my understanding about God and just who He was. *Proverbs 14:12 says, "There is a way that seems right to man."*

It was while I was attending Cerritos College in 1976, studying to become an accountant, that Jesus changed my life and this wrong way of thinking. I was going to school during the day and working part-time in a small machine shop in Paramount, California. I was going to parties and lots of dance clubs all over Southern California almost every night, drinking cheap wine and smoking marijuana. My friends and I were completely caught up in the culture of the '70s. One of the standard sayings of that day was, "Keep on truckin'." That is exactly what we were doing: living and loving this carefree lifestyle.

The Vietnam War was the only threat to my college commitment. I was ready any day to be drafted and sent off to fight for our country. I was living at home with my parents rent-free. My parents paid my auto insurance, most of my school expenses, food, and even the gas for my car, a 1962 Ford van that they had also purchased. I had it all.

I never gave much thought to things like religion, church, growing up, and being an adult. Pretty much all I cared about was myself and a few close friends.

My first girlfriend in school was my first love and brought me to my life's big crossroad—I emphasize the "CROSS" in the road. She and I were together through most of junior high and some of senior high school, but broke up just before my junior year. My friends used to tease me because I talked about her all the time.

Do you remember your first love? They say "Your first car is like your first love, you will never forget them!" We experimented with pot together while we were going steady. Except for a couple of tries of a very strong drug called angel dust, which I was told afterward is some kind of animal tranquilizer that stays in your brain for years, I never went on to use any other drugs. However, my girlfriend did go on to stronger and more dangerous drugs.

One morning in January, I got up to go to work and my mother told me that my former girlfriend was very sick and in the hospital. I decided to go after work and pay her a visit, not aware of how sick she really was. When I got there she was tied to the bed, tubes in every part of her body, hooked up to all kinds of machines with lights, bells and beeping sounds. She was in the final stages of Hepatitis C. Her eyes and skin were yellow and she could barely speak. I could not believe what I was seeing. My very first love was dying right in front of me. There was nothing I could do; I was totally helpless to help her.

I did not know how to pray, and I didn't know God in any way, shape, or form. She was barely able to communicate, but through her slurred words she asked me to read to her. I was fresh out of reading material, so I grabbed the book that is in most hospital rooms: a Gideon Bible. So with all the expertise of a "not-so-great first-year Bible student," I opened to a book called John. I can't remember much of what I read, but it seemed to give her some comfort.

After I left the room, I completely came apart. Totally uncontrolled tears ran down my face and a feeling of being more lost than I have ever felt in my life overcame me.

The next day when I went to see her, I stopped first at a flower shop across the street from the hospital. I was weeping so much that the lady couldn't understand what I was asking for. She guessed my emotion and cried herself at my grief. I come by these tears naturally and I am in good company as Jeremiah was known as the "Weeping Prophet," and John tells of Jesus weeping for Lazarus at his death.

As I walked into the room with flowers in hand, I was surprised to see that my ex-girlfriend was sitting up in a chair, not as yellow or as sick. She seemed to be getting better. Our communication was clearer, and we visited a couple of hours. She wanted me to read to her again. Again, I got the Bible and read some more, not understanding it one bit better. Two unbelievers reaching out to God for help, and we wouldn't have known what to do with that divine help if we got it. God would save both of us, although not in a way either of us could or would understand for some time. Jesus, in His infinite wisdom, knew perfectly what each of us needed.

Her salvation came the next day, by way of her death, mine after her funeral. A young man shared the gospel with me after her funeral. He said he had remembered seeing my girlfriend at several services before she got sick. He thought she had told him that she had asked Jesus into her life and that may be why she wanted me to read from the Bible. Only God knows. This young man took the time to explain to me that God sent His Son into the world in human form to save mankind—and me. He patiently answered my questions about the Bible, God, death, and most importantly, my grief.

That night when I was alone with all the thoughts of that dark and terrible day, I prayed "Jesus, I don't know if I can live this new life with You, but if You will forgive me, I promise to trust You with all my heart." At that very moment on my bed in the middle of the night, I felt the weight of that dreadful day and my whole life lift up from my soul. It felt like I rose up from my bed and floated when Jesus came into my life. I've never been the same and never wanted to return to the past life. I started reading the Bible the next day in the weirdest place for a new Christian to start reading.

God's plan was for me to read a very special verse, *Revelation 2:4: "Nevertheless I have this against you, that you have left your first love."* God came into my life because I thought I had lost my very first love. God in His Bible was telling me two things: my first love is really Jesus Christ and He loves me much more than I could ever love anyone else in my life.

The next step in my life was entering into the family of God by way of the church. About six months later, I was asked by my brother to go on a blind date. My date's family went to a church in Bell Gardens.

The next day was Sunday, and I asked her if I could meet her at her church, and she said yes; so I went to my first Sunday school class and a worship service. This became my home church and is to this day.

We dated for two years and during that dating time, we got engaged. I would come to find that my new wife was the perfect example of a Proverbs 31 woman. We got married September 16, 1978, in our home church and have been married for over thirty-four years! I can't believe that she has been able to put up with me for all these years. God did not bless us with children of our own, but He provided many opportunities for us to work with the youth groups from the church and community.

In fact, I became a junior high Sunday school teacher and then started working as a youth pastor with the junior high kids. I eventually became the senior high youth pastor and an associate pastor.

Wow, what a great story of salvation — so far.

But like the famous Paul Harvey would say: And now, the rest of the story ...

My addiction to gambling started very slowly. One night after our Wednesday youth meeting, I asked my new assistant youth leader to go to dinner with me at a restaurant in Downey, California. While we were seated at a table waiting for our waitress to take our order, I noticed a numbered game panel on one of the TV screens near our table. As we watched the graphics, little white balls would float across the multicolored game board and light on one number at a time, a lot like BINGO. I asked my friend what it was and he said it was called Keno, a legal gambling game new to California. I had been to Las Vegas a few times in my life, and even played Keno there along with many other games of chance. I always lost my money pretty easily, but had a lot of fun.

I never realized how much my need to gamble was addicting, because it was always so far to go to Vegas to play. I was never comfortable in the local poker casinos, so I didn't consider them to be a temptation for me. But these local restaurants and 7 – 11's were right up my alley, so to speak. They were simple and easy gambling establishments, fun places to get involved in a very wrong way of spending my hard-earned money. Slowly but surely, I spent more and more money for my addiction. Some of that money was supposed to be for bills and everyday expenses. I started getting money out of our checking and saving accounts. I actually depleted our savings account two times. I was caught by my wife many times and, of course, I promised I would stop. My "stopping" was really my sick way of thinking "getting money without being caught" by my wife.

I was a textbook example of a full-blown addict; I needed my "gambling fix" just like a person hooked on any other kind of habit. And I exhibited all the behaviors that go along with addictions: stealing, lying, denial, and just plain being too proud to admit I had an out-of-control habit.

My life was in a downward spiral. While at work, church, or home, I made out that I was living up to the principles taught from the Bible. But in my alone times, with no accountability, I was in the uncontrolled addiction of my struggle. I was spending money and using funds that were meant to buy food, gas, and pay bills. I was in love with trying to be the next winner, no matter how much it cost.

In 2008, my wife called me at work and asked the deadly question, "Have you been gambling again? There is a lot of money missing from our accounts." I admitted how out-of-control I was, and how sorry I was, and that it would never happen again. Translated: "I'll try to control my gambling and hide it better to not get caught." In *1 John 1:8–10* the Bible reminds me that *"If we say we have no sin, we are only fooling ourselves, and refusing to accept the truth. But if we confess our sins to him, he can be depended on to forgive us and cleanse us from every wrong. If we claim we have not sinned, we are lying and calling God a liar, for he says we all have sinned."* Although I admitted to my wife that I had messed up, I was not willing to admit it to God or to confess my sins to Him.

As you can imagine, my wife saw right through this lame excuse because she had a very close friend who was in 12 Step meetings and could tell when an addict was lying. My wife informed me she had found a Gamblers Anonymous meeting on Saturday nights in Downey, and I needed to attend or else. I went and was involved with that organization for about a year. My accountability to the meeting was enough to make me stop for over a year, but it was just another "white-knuckle experience." I truly spoke every Saturday night about my struggle by saying "Hi, my name is Monty and I haven't placed a bet in over a year." Accountability really works, but after a year, I felt like I was cured. So, I stopped going to the meetings and within a few weeks, I would spend two or three dollars on scratchers or a couple of games of Keno. In just a short time, I was back in as deep as before. Still being a practicing Christian and a practicing gambler every chance I would get.

On April 9, 2010, I got that bitter call from my wife. Again! I knew this time it was the "or else." But after many strong warnings and a time of clarity, we decided it was time to look for a Christian recovery program.

This time, she located a Christ-centered recovery program called Celebrate Recovery. I was informed that my choice was: to go on Friday, or I could go on Friday. She left it up to me.

I went to Celebrate Recovery that Friday. I started going to the groups, and the change came almost from the first night when I told my wife this is truly a Christ-involved program. I was welcomed, loved on, and felt the presence of the Holy Spirit when I entered those rooms the first time!

Since coming to Celebrate Recovery, my life has been changed in more ways than I could have ever dreamed of or hoped for. The program was filled with many helpful tools to guide me into a wonderful transition from guilt, lying, and bad behaviors to forgiveness, honesty, good habits, new friendships, and a brand-new relationship with our God, His church, and the Bible.

After attending a few meetings, my new friends told me about another great tool in Celebrate Recovery called a step study group and how it had changed their lives both physically and more importantly, spiritually. I decided to take the leap of faith and began attending a step study group at Emmanuel Church. The real teacher is God's Holy Spirit. Through the Word of God and the step study participant's guides, which are based upon the eight principles, I've learned more about God's great love and care for my hurts, hang-ups, and habits.

Principle 7 says, "Reserve a daily time with God for self-examination,

Bible reading, and prayer in order to know God and His will for my life and gain the power to follow His will."

I've learned to trust the wisdom of my heavenly Father to make me into a new creature filled with truth, love, and grace, and to walk in the newness of life promised by our wonderful Redeemer.

Second Corinthians 5:17 states, "Therefore, if anyone is in Christ, he is a new creation; the old has gone, the new has come!"

As the weeks and months passed, the step study became more and more a part of my everyday life. My friends, family, and coworkers have noticed the changes in me, and I didn't have to tell them. By the grace of God and applying the eight principles based on the Beatitudes, I have not gambled since April 9, 2010. This is a miracle and now I know what people mean when they say, "Don't leave before the miracle happens." God has replaced my need to gamble with a need to know Him and His Word. The Holy Spirit is leading me "one day at a time," and I am definitely "enjoying every moment at a time."

I would like to share a Scripture that has helped me on this road to recovery: *"For as many as are led by the Spirit of God, these are sons of God. For you did not receive the spirit of bondage again to fear, but you received the Spirit of adoption by whom we cry out, 'Abba, Father.' The Spirit himself bears witness with our spirit that we are children of God, and if children, then heirs—heirs of God and joint heirs with Christ, if indeed we suffer with him, that we may also be glorified together" (Romans 8:14–17).*

I know that God is on this road to recovery with me, and He is helping me every day to stay out of my mess. My work in the church is one area that has benefited because of my attendance at Celebrate Recovery. I'm much more effective as an assistant pastor, teacher, and shepherd. Even in my home I am becoming the kind of man my wife deserves by being the husband God wanted me to be all along.

God bless you and God bless Celebrate Recovery!

Thank you for letting me share.

Principle 8

> **Principle 8:** Yield myself to God to be used to bring this Good News to others, both by my example and by my words.
>
> *"Happy are those who are persecuted because they do what God requires." (Matthew 5:10)*

Major, miraculous progress and growth will have occurred in your life since you started your recovery program, since you began working Principle 1. You will have stepped out of your denial into God's grace. You will have taken an honest spiritual inventory. Worked on getting right with God, yourself, and others. And most of all, you will have grown in your relationship with Christ. Discovered a new way to live life, and you will be finding the serenity you have always sought. But the most exciting part is yet to come—in Principle 8.

Principle 8 is the "giving back" principle. It's about giving back because we *want* to, not because we *have* to. We want to share the freedom and victory God has given us with others who are still trapped in their hurts, hang-ups, and habits.

What is giving back all about? What does it truly mean to give? First of all, Principle 8 doesn't ask us to give in unhealthy ways, ways that might hurt us or cause us to relapse into our old, codependent behaviors. No, Principle 8 is all about healthy, non-codependent giving of ourselves—giving freely, without the slightest expectation that we will receive anything in return. No one has ever been honored, after all, for what they've received. Honor has always been a reward to those who gave.

Matthew 10:8 sums up the heart of Principle 8: "Freely you have received; freely give."

Once we understand how to freely give of ourselves in healthy ways, we can start living the eighth principle, and in particular Step 12 of the Christ-centered 12 Steps.

Step 12: Having had a spiritual experience as the result of these steps, we tried to carry this message to others and to practice these principles in all our affairs.

"Brothers, if someone is caught in a sin, you who are spiritual should restore him gently. But watch yourself, or you also may be tempted."
(Galatians 6:1)

Sometimes we get to Principle 8 and feel as though we really don't have anything to offer someone else. We feel as though we're not worthy of helping another person, that we're not eligible to be used by God in this way. Nothing could be further from the truth.

As an example, take an old, beat-up soft drink can—dirty, dented, even squashed. A few years ago, it would have been thrown into the garbage and deemed useless, of no continuing value. Modern technology has changed that. Today it can be recycled, melted down, purified, and made into a new can—shiny and clean—that can be used again.

That's what Principle 8 does. It recycles our pain by allowing God's fire and light to shine on it—to melt down our old hurts, hang-ups, and habits so we can be used again in a positive way. Our lives can be recycled to show others how we've worked the principles and steps, with Jesus' healing, and how we've come through the darkness of our pain into Christ's glorious freedom and light.

Society tells us that pain is useless. In fact, some people believe that *people* in pain are useless. At Celebrate Recovery, we know that pain has value, as do the people who experience it. So while the world says no, Principle 8 shouts a resounding YES:

Yield myself to God.
Example is important.
Serve others as Jesus Christ did.

The road to recovery leads to service. Some will choose to serve at Celebrate Recovery. Others will prefer to devote their skills to other areas in the church.

We need to share our experiences, victories, and hopes with newcomers. We do that as leaders, sponsors, and accountability partners. But the church also needs our service. As we lend a hand outside Celebrate Recovery, we can share with others and motivate them to get into recovery when they're ready to face their own hurts, hang-ups, and habits.

The world is populated by two kinds of people—givers and takers. The takers eat well, but the givers sleep well. Be a giver. There are many, many areas in which to serve. Make suggestions. Get involved.

Principle 8 comes down to this: Do what you can with what you have from where you are. Make your life a mission, not an intermission.

Live out Principles 7 and 8 on a daily basis for the remainder of your time on this earth, and your life will be full and rewarding as you follow God's purpose for you.

Every morning, before you get out of bed, pray this prayer:

Principle 8 Prayer

Dear Jesus, as it would please You, bring me someone today whom I can serve. Amen.

PRINCIPLE 8 TESTIMONY

My name is Mac, and I am a grateful believer in Jesus Christ who struggles with drug and alcohol addiction. I have lived to see a milestone in my recovery. After twenty-four years in recovery, I've finally been sober longer than I was using.

My childhood was pretty uneventful in terms of abuse. My parents loved me and set good standards to live by. So I can't look back to blame others for my actions, actions that brought great shame. Today because of Jesus Christ, I don't have to live in the past anymore. I am free!

Ironically though, I spent a lifetime searching for freedom in all the wrong things. My dad was in the military, so by the time I was fifteen, I had moved eight times. I learned to blend in and make friends quickly.

My dad preached wherever he was stationed. So I knew about God, heaven, and hell. I was taught that unless you were a Christian you would go to hell. I remember fear being the motivating factor for being baptized when I was twelve. I appeared to enter a relationship with God, but for all the wrong reasons. Two weeks later at summer camp, I was introduced to marijuana by one of the counselors. I found a group of people who looked like they were having a lot of fun, so I decided, "Who needs to live in fear? These people aren't worrying about anything!" I became fearless and believed I was invincible, not realizing I had set the pace for eventual destruction.

My dad retired from the military and went to seminary to become a full-time pastor, so we moved to Louisiana when I was fifteen. I hated the fact that we were moving and I wondered how I would ever find friends who liked doing what I liked to do now. Amazingly within the first week, I found the same people there. I never ran out of drugs, and acceptance was immediate.

Once we arrived, my parents sent me to church summer camp to straighten me out and that's where I met Mary.

Mary: My name is Mary. I am a grateful believer in Jesus Christ who struggles with codependency.

I grew up an elder's kid. My parents lived out the Deuteronomy verse: "to tie God's word as symbols around your hands and teach them to your children as you walk by them day after day." There were always guests at the dinner table in our home. Missionaries from foreign countries stayed with us for recharging, while others flocked to our home seeking wise counsel, Bible study, and to repair wrecked marriages.

During my childhood, my mother would write Bible verses on three-by-five cards and tape them up all over our bathroom walls. As I would get dressed in the morning, there staring me in the face would be several verses I would read over and over. It just became a habit without me even realizing it. My sister and I would throw our heads under the covers at night and giggle, thinking how silly it was having our mama reciting those verses to us, never realizing the impact they would have on me in years to come.

I confessed Jesus as Lord of my life when I was twelve years old and was baptized telling myself, "I would *never* sin again!" I wanted to please God with all my heart.

Mac: A new school year began; Mary was a senior and I was a junior. Life was great! After a few months of dating, I talked her into having sex, the first time for both of us, by using the manipulative "if you love me" line. Two weeks later, she didn't start her period, but we thought, *No way; surely one time can't get you pregnant.*

Mary: Four months later I finally consulted a doctor and, yes, I was pregnant. No one had been pregnant outside of marriage in our church, so we had a secret. I felt alone and was convinced Mac couldn't support us. He was only sixteen at the time.

By the time I was five months pregnant, I decided it was confession time to my dad. During my childhood, my mother had a mental illness. Doctors put her through experimental procedures such as electric shock treatments. She suffered in mental hospitals and was a test subject for drugs that often kept her debilitated. So needless to say, my sweet mother who loved me the best she knew how didn't notice I had a growing belly.

I had always been able to talk to my dad, and I knew I couldn't keep it from him any longer. I walked into the den where my dad was taking a nap. I had snuggled up next to him many times throughout the years on that big old flowered sofa, while he read Bible stories to me and we talked about God's love. I knelt down next to him, eye to eye, and said softly, "We need to talk, Daddy."

I was prepared for him to point his finger and say all kinds of harsh words.

But tears began streaming down his cheeks as he said he

would support and love me always. I told him my plans for moving out of town and giving my baby up for adoption.

I left home for my secret summer trip. Three months later it was August 17, 1975. That date is significant later in our story. The doctor left me in a tiny room all alone. Labor lasted for twelve hours with no anesthesia and no family. As they rushed me into the delivery room, a nurse shoved a gas mask over my face. I thought they were suffocating me to punish me for what I had done.

I awoke later in bed sheets soaking wet from perspiration and tears. I experienced emotions that were alien to me. A time that was supposed to be the happiest time of my life was my saddest. I moved to a Christian college out of state. My dad was hoping to get me away from Mac.

Mac: But I followed her there. My parents thought by sending me to a Christian college, they would fix me. Guess what? I found the people who loved to party my first day on campus. In fact, I found the guy who first introduced me to pot six years earlier at church camp. Halfway through the semester, I was kicked out of college after sneaking out of the dorm past curfew to smoke a joint with a friend. Mary and I both went home and married three weeks later.

Married life was great. We partied all the time. Later we would come to understand it helped us to mask the guilt of giving up our baby. When we had been married three years, we started trying to have another baby. Mary told me she was quitting the partying. I said, "Go ahead, but I'm not." Even in the midst of my addiction, I set a boundary and decided to quit everything except smoking pot. I convinced myself that marijuana wasn't so bad.

As I continued down the road of drug addiction, the conflict began between us. Our two daughters were born during this time. However, we lived separate lives under the same roof while growing further apart. I stayed away from the house as much as possible, working overtime to pay for my drug habit. By this time, meth had become my drug of choice.

Mary: In time, I came to the realization that our marriage was totally unmanageable, and I couldn't survive without turning my life and hurts over to God. I had to quit trying to be Mac's Holy Spirit and fix him and instead work on my own shortcomings. I started seeking the pathway to peace while Mac continued to run down the path to destruction. This pattern continued for seven years.

I held on to the verses I remembered reading as a child on my bathroom wall. *In Isaiah 55:11, it says when God's word is spoken; it does not come back empty but will accomplish what He desires and achieve the purpose for which He sent it.*

I would also repeat *Isaiah 41:10* to myself the way I remembered my mother quoted it, slowly and distinctly. I felt God was speaking to me.

"Do not fear for I am with you. Do not be afraid for I am your God. I will strengthen you and help you. I will uphold you with my righteous right hand."

All those Scriptures I heard as a child were coming back to me, comforting me during the dark and lonely nights. Now I had two secrets I carried. We had a son we would never know and I had an insane husband! I say insane because I didn't know all the drugs he was doing and their effects.

So I walked on eggshells to keep peace. I wore my mask to church every Sunday. I just wanted my insides to feel like everyone else looked on the outside: perfect, I thought.

Mac: Amazingly enough, even as a drug addict, there was a line I said I would never cross. The last two years of my addiction I was shooting up ten to twelve times a day. I wore long-sleeve shirts all the time so no one would notice the marks on my arms. I slept only about sixteen hours a week. One Sunday morning, God gave me a great gift at the time and I didn't even realize it. It was a moment of clarity.

I was crashed out in the bed, and our four-year-old daughter stood beside the bed and said to her mother, "Why doesn't Daddy go to church with us anymore?" Mary said, "He's been working hard. He needs sleep." Our daughter replied, "If he doesn't go to church, then I'm not either!" I pretended to be asleep and not hear what she said.

They left for church and then all of a sudden I felt like I ran into a brick wall. God used a little girl to break my heart. I realized I was killing everybody I claimed to love. It was as if my eyes were opened for the first time seeing the insanity of it all. So I collected all my drugs and paraphernalia and burned them.

Mary: I was crushed realizing our children were being affected. That Sunday the sermon was on confession and how good it is for the soul. I remember the song "It Is Well with My Soul." The words hung in my throat. I couldn't breathe. I wanted to just run out of the building. Arriving home, I found Mac sitting in his recliner with tears in his eyes.

Mac: I was raised to believe that men shouldn't cry or show any weakness. But what I found in those tears that morning was relief like I'd never known. I told Mary all that I had done and that I wanted to start a new life. For the first time, Mary stepped out of her codependency and said,

Mary: "Who are you going to call? I'm tired of keeping secrets."

Mac: "I told you I'm through with that life. What more do you want?"

Mary: "We need someone to help us. Would you talk to our pastor?"

Mac: Our pastor had been coming to my cabinet shop for years, getting me to build things for him, only to find out later they were things he really didn't need. He saw something in me that nobody else did. So he came over to pray with us. He said I didn't have to confess before the church, but I might help someone else if I did. I knew I needed to be held accountable.

Mary and I responded to an altar call that Sunday night, expecting to be shunned by people. The whole church came down afterward and cried with us. They didn't know what to do with me—I was their first drug addict—but they loved me and said to keep coming back.

There was one lady who said I needed to go to AA. I thought she was talking about some kind of car club. She said, "Not triple A, but double A—Alcoholics Anonymous."

Mary wanted me to talk to someone at a rehab center the next day. I told her I wasn't crazy and didn't need that. I finally agreed to talk but nothing more. After much discussion with the head guy, he asked if I would stay. I said, "Okay, I guess I'll stay. But I've got to go home and get my stuff."

Mary: "That's okay; your stuff is in the trunk!"

Mac: Our life became a whirlwind with rehab, ninety meetings in ninety days, Bible studies, and making new friends. A whole new life had begun for us. We started Overcomers two years later, which we led for fourteen years. We had approximately twenty to thirty people who came on a regular basis.

Mary: The only other people who knew about our son were my dad, my brother, and his wife. Fast-forward to spring 1988, one month after Mac yielded to God, when God gave us a surprise gift. Our church youth group was going to a rally five hours away and my sister-in-law was one of the chaperones.

They were assigning groups to stay in homes and by the time they got to my sister-in-law's group, they had run out of homes. So they were asked if they would mind staying in a town close by. As the suitcases were being loaded into the car of a friendly couple, my sister-in-law asked if they had any children. When the woman said they had a son named Heath, a funny feeling came over my sister-in-law. So she asked his age. Heath's mother said he was twelve. So my sister-in-law went one step further and asked, "When is his birthday?" Heath's mother said August 17—the date our firstborn, Heath, arrived on August 17, 1975!

At 2:00 a.m. our phone rang. My sister-in-law whispered, "You'll never imagine where I am." I said sleepily, "Where?" She replied, "Heath's bed!" A family at our church has the last name, Heath, so I questioned her, "What are you doing in Mr. Heath's bed?" She exclaimed, "No, no—Heath, *your son*!" Mac and I feel

God gave us that gift at that time in our lives to reassure us our son was loved and cared for in a Christian home.

After waiting seven more years, in August 1994 we got the call we always hoped we would get. When Heath was about to turn nineteen, his parents contacted us and said that he would like to meet us on his birthday. My dad was in charge of videoing the momentous occasion, but as we sat down later to view it, the whole first part of the reunion video was showing the ground. My dad was so excited he forgot he was holding the camera!

It's been seventeen years now since we first met Heath. We didn't get to see Heath's natural birth, but we were blessed with witnessing his spiritual birth as Mac baptized him! In 2005, Heath's parents moved to our city and Heath's mother and my mom became best friends as she took care of my mom after my dad died. We also attend the same church and celebrate holidays together. Our family continues to grow as God has blessed us now with eight grandchildren!

Mac: After leading Overcomers Outreach for thirteen years, Mary's brother "happened" to be at Saddleback Church and told me about a ministry called Celebrate Recovery and said I ought to check it out. So in 2004, we attended the Summit. During the second day I told Mary, "We're stopping what we're doing and starting this! Look how many more people we can help—more than just drug addicts and alcoholics, anyone with a hurt, habit, or hang-up!" After 120 days of prayer and preparation, we started Celebrate Recovery at our church on New Year's Eve 2004! During this preparation time, I learned about Principle 8 and realized that this is exactly what God had in mind for us.

Principle 8 states: "Yield myself to God to be used to bring this good news to others, both by my example and by my words." "Happy are those who are persecuted because they do what God requires" (Matthew 5:10).

This is why we went through all of these trials and then we found out there was more!

I love watching God's plan for our life unfold. A few years

ago, a pastor of forty years tried to commit suicide. The "Phari-sees" in the church finally got to him. And the only way he could get through his week was by doing something he said he would never do—take a drink. That one drink turned into every Mon-day. He had been drinking the last ten years and nobody knew except his wife. Finally he couldn't take the hypocrisy of his own life anymore and that's when he attempted suicide. Along with the bottle, he took a handful of pills. He was moved from pastor to one of "those" people. So I got the call to go visit him.

I visited him in the ICU and even though he was uncon-scious, I prayed over him and said, "Don't give up. God still has a plan for you." Over the next few weeks, I was able to share with him about the hope that God still had for him. He later became a part of our Celebrate Recovery ministry. While at one of our small groups, he shared with me that he had just met our son's parents at church on Sunday. I said, "Everybody has; they go to church here now!" And he said, "No, no, you don't understand. Forty years ago when I first became a pastor I performed their marriage ceremony!" Before our son was conceived, God had a plan to use this man to marry the couple that would adopt our son! And then later, allow me to be instrumental in giving him the hope that his relationship could not only be restored, but also that God would continue to use him! God always sees the big picture, and He is always right on time!

Mary: We went from the twenty to thirty people attending our Overcomers' group, a ministry that was already working, to an average attendance of over 250 every Friday night at Celebrate Recovery. Our children are a part of Celebrate Recovery. They serve in roles of state rep, ministry leader, training coach, open share group leaders, nursery worker, videographer, and youth minister.

Twenty-four years ago, I prayed God would just keep Mac awake in church. God has truly taken the ashes of our lives and turned them into something beautiful. I believe when God said in *Joel 2:25, "I will repay you for the years the locusts have eaten."*

We can't keep quiet about what the Lord has done in our lives and in the lives of our Celebrate Recovery Forever Family! If there is restoration for us, there is hope for you too! Don't give up; put your faith in action by making life's healing choices.

Mac: Being on the front line of what I believe is THE outreach ministry of the church, we are able to bind up the brokenhearted, to proclaim freedom for the captives of sin in Jesus' name, and release from darkness the prisoners of hurts, hang-ups, and habits.

Celebrate Recovery has helped us reach more hurting people to find healing than we could've ever imagined. How can we repay the Lord for His goodness! We share the hope we've found in Jesus! Today we are making life's healing choices and that's Celebrate Recovery!

Thank you for letting us share.

Chapter 3

WHAT CAN I EXPECT TO HAPPEN AT MY FIRST CELEBRATE RECOVERY MEETING?

A simple reply to that question is a lot! But before we answer in detail, it might be helpful to give you an overview of a typical Celebrate Recovery meeting.

A typical Celebrate Recovery meeting includes:

- A pre-meeting dinner
- A large group meeting
- An open share small group
- Newcomers 101 (for your first week only)

Participants are encouraged to invite their families and friends to the pre-meeting dinner if they so choose; the dinner is designed for a time of great fellowship and great food at affordable prices with other Celebrate Recovery participants.

The large group meeting is designed for the participant to set aside the busyness and stress of the outside world by entering into a time of prayer, praise and worship, and teaching as a way of getting in touch with the one and only Higher Power, Jesus Christ.

The open share small group meets immediately after the large group meeting and provides a place for the participant to connect with other Celebrate Recovery attendees. This is a safe place where participants can be in gender-specific groups and issue-specific groups.

Newcomers 101 is for first-time attendees and will help you better understand what Celebrate Recovery is all about as well as provide you the opportunity to ask questions or process your feelings in a safe environment before you make a commitment to a small group.

After you've attended Celebrate Recovery for a while, you will join a step study. The step study small group is for those who are ready to delve deeper into their past and the choices they have made. This is where participants will see real, lasting changes start to happen. Step studies take place another night of the week.

Now let's take a closer look at the components of each meeting on any given night at Celebrate Recovery.

The Pre-Meeting Dinner

At Saddleback, the evening usually starts off with a dinner around 6:00 p.m. Times and menus might vary for different Celebrate Recovery locations. We serve a Bar-B-Que at our program that runs from 6:00 to 7:00 p.m. You can choose from the following menu items:

Recovery Dog Dinner
12-Step Chicken
Serenity Sausage
Or a Denial Burger
With 60-Day Chips and
Keep Coming Back Onions

This event provides great fellowship and great food at very affordable prices. For the recovery dog dinner, which includes a hot dog, soda, chips, and salad, we only charge $2.50. Watch out, McDonald's!

For four months of the year (due to the severe winters we have in Southern California!), we shut down the Bar-B-Que and have an inside pizza dinner. We encourage you to invite your friends and family.

Large Group Meeting Format: Worship and Teaching Time

At 7:00 p.m. we begin our "large group" worship and teaching time.

During the large group time, everyone meets together—all the men and women combined. This time is designed to help everyone to focus by participating in a twenty-minute time of prayer, praise, and worship.

> *"Praise the LORD. Praise God in his sanctuary; praise him in his mighty heavens. Praise him for his acts of power; praise him for his surpassing greatness. Praise him with the sounding of the trumpet, praise him with the harp and lyre, praise him with timbrel and dancing, praise him with the strings and pipe, praise him with the clash of cymbals, praise him with resounding cymbals. Let everything that has breath praise the LORD. Praise the LORD."* (Psalm 150:1–6)

It also includes a time for teaching a lesson from the *Celebrate Recovery Leader's Guide* or a testimony of a "changed life." This time begins to unfold the **safe** environment that is essential to any recovery program. It allows all of us to get in touch with the one and only Higher Power, Jesus Christ.

The evening typically follows this agenda:

6:30 p.m.: Doors open

As you come into the meeting, the greeters will hand you the Celebrate Recovery bulletin for the evening (see box on page 96).

The Celebrate Recovery Bulletin

The bulletin contains the following information:

- Song sheet of words (unless they are projected on screen)
- Solid Rock Cafe/Bar-B-Que information sheets
- Small group meeting guidelines
- Eight recovery principles and the Christ-centered 12 Steps
- Twelve Steps and their biblical comparisons
- List of all the open share groups that are meeting that night and room assignments
- List of the open step study small groups that meet during the week
- Announcements of upcoming special events
- Prayer request sheets
- Serenity Prayer

7:00 p.m.: Opening song, welcome, and opening prayer

We attempt to begin our large group meeting promptly at 7:00 p.m. and end by 8:00 p.m. This will ensure that you have a full hour for your small group meetings that meet from 8:00 to 9:00 p.m. After the first song, someone on the leadership team welcomes everyone and prays the opening prayer.

7:05 p.m.: Praise and worship

The music continues with songs chosen to go along with the particular principle we will be working on that evening. This praise and worship time is extremely important! We encourage everyone to participate. But if you are not comfortable doing so, you can remain seated. We completely understand.

7:20 p.m.: Reading of the Eight Recovery Principles or the Christ-centered 12 Steps

Two individuals are selected to read the eight principles or the 12 Steps. The purpose is twofold: (1) to reinforce the biblical foundation of the program, and (2) to allow increased participation for Celebrate Recovery leaders. The opportunity to read is used to recognize leaders and encourage prospective new coleaders.

One person is asked to read the principle/step and another reads the Bible verse for that principle/step until all eight principles/12 Steps are completed.

Example:

> *First reader:* "Principle 1: Realize I'm not God. I admit that I am powerless to control my tendency to do the wrong thing and that my life is unmanageable."
>
> *Second reader:* "Happy are those who know they are spiritually poor." (Matthew 5:3 GNT)

7:25 p.m.: Celebrate Recovery news

The purpose of the Celebrate Recovery news is to help you feel welcome and informed. You will hear about the special group for newcomers where you can get your questions answered — Celebrate Recovery Newcomers 101.

While the Celebrate Recovery news is an important part of the program, announcements can be rather "dry," so we attempt to make them light and fun. The remainder of the time is used to announce upcoming events at church and Celebrate Recovery and to introduce the "special music" for the evening.

7:30 p.m.: Special music

Special music supports the teaching or the testimony for the evening. It is usually a solo performed by one of the Celebrate Recovery singers. Also, during the special music selection, a collection, or "love offering," may be taken. The money collected could be used to support child-care, to pay for special speakers, and to offset regular expenses. *We make it clear that no one is obligated to give to this offering!*

7:35 p.m.: Teaching or testimony

The speaker will teach one of the twenty-five lessons from the

Celebrate Recovery Leader's Guide. Typically, the next week follows with a testimony which supports the teaching of the previous week's lesson.

7:55 p.m.: Serenity Prayer and dismissal to open share groups
The large group meeting ends with one of the leaders leading the group in the reading of the complete version of Reinhold Niebuhr's Serenity Prayer. The prayer is printed on the inside cover of the bulletin jacket. Then we sing the closing song and everyone is encouraged to quickly go to their small group meetings located throughout the church campus. Meeting locations are also noted in the bulletin. If you have questions, you can stop by the Celebrate Recovery information table or ask one of the Celebrate Recovery leaders. The leaders are easy for you to spot because they wear a Celebrate Recovery leader's shirt or lanyard.

Celebrate Recovery's Small Group Formats
Open Share Small Group
These small groups meet immediately after the large group concludes. There are separate groups for men and women. The format is as follows:

8:00 p.m.: Opening prayer, welcome, introductions, and guidelines
When you enter the room you will find the seats arranged in a circle. Feel free to sit in any of the open seats.

The leader will welcome everyone and then say, *"Good evening. My name is _____; I am a believer who struggles with _____."*

The reason we introduce ourselves this way ("I'm a believer …") is that our identity is in Jesus Christ—the One and only Higher Power. Then we go on to say, "who struggles with _____." Our struggles are not our identity! Our struggles are our hurts, hang-ups, habits, and sins. But you and I are children of God!

You may be wondering, "Do I have to believe in God and Jesus to participate in Celebrate Recovery?" The answer is "absolutely not." All that we ask is that you keep your heart and mind open. Outside of the group, if you ask, your leader will be happy to talk to you about what it means to make the decision to ask Christ into your life!

The leader then says, *"Let's take a minute now to introduce ourselves. I'll begin, and we'll go around the room. Again my name is _____; I'm a believer who struggles with _____."*

You can do the same, or if you are not ready to make that statement you can simply say, *"I'm _____."*

Don't be surprised that after each person introduces himself or herself, the group will respond by saying, *"Hi _____"* back to you.

The leader then says, *"Before we open the meeting for sharing, we have the reading of the small group guidelines.* (Note: The five small group guidelines can be found on page 104.) *These guidelines are designed to provide a safe and productive meeting for everyone. Please listen carefully and honor these guidelines throughout the meeting."*

8:05 p.m.: Leader's focus on the principle

The leader starts the group's sharing by reading the focus question from the large group lesson. If there was a testimony that evening, the leader could ask the group to focus on what part of the testimony touched them the most.

8:10 p.m.: Group open sharing

This is the heart of the small group time. Everyone can choose to share on the focus question or just feel free to share whatever is on their hearts. Remember, you have the guidelines to keep your sharing safe! If you do not feel ready to share, that is not a problem. All you have to do is say, "Pass." You will find that as the weeks go by, you will be sharing! Just keep coming back!

8:50 p.m.: Wrap-up and closing prayer
Wrapping up the session is the leader's responsibility. It is up to the leader to see that the group has enough time for closure—that the meeting does not just come to an abrupt halt or go on and on and on.

9:00 p.m.: Invitation to the Solid Rock Cafe
The meeting can now continue "unofficially" at the Solid Rock Cafe, a place designed specifically for fellowship. At the cafe, you have an opportunity to continue to share with those with whom you feel safe. This, like the dinner before the meeting, is a time for you to continue developing accountability partners and sponsorship relationships.

Step Study Small Groups

The step study groups are the second type of Celebrate Recovery small groups. This is where you delve deeper into your past and the choices you have made. This is where you will see real, lasting changes start to happen in your life! Quite honestly, at first you may not be able to see the changes God is making in your life. But others will start seeing the changes in you. This is the beginning of restoring relationships!

Don't worry: you do not need to join a step study group in your first week. In fact, I suggest you keep attending the large group and your open share small group for at least three to six months before you consider joining a step study.

By then, you will have formed your accountability team. They can help you decide when you are ready!

Step study groups meet on a different night of the week from the large group and open share group meetings. The step study groups go though the four Celebrate Recovery participant's guides together. It usually takes the group about a year to complete them. You will answer and discuss the questions at the end of each lesson together. The group will close (i.e., no new participants) after they have completed the lessons on the third principle. There are separate groups for men and women.

The typical step study group agenda is as follows:

7:00 p.m.	Opening prayer and welcome
	Introductions
	Serenity Prayer
	Reading of the eight principles and/or the 12 Steps and their biblical comparisons
	Reading of Celebrate Recovery's small group meeting guidelines
	Leader's focus on the principle or topic
7:15 p.m.	Group discussion of that night's lesson from the participant's guide. (The leader will go around the group and let everyone have a chance to share their answer to *each question.* Depending on the size of your step study, it may take two weeks to cover one lesson.
8:50 p.m.	Wrap-up, prayer requests, closing prayer
9:00 p.m.	Closing

A Comparison of the Three Celebrate Recovery Groups

The following illustration will help you see the components of each of the three types of Celebrate Recovery groups: large group, open share small group, and the step study small group.

Large Group

- Worship
- Read the steps or principles
- Announcements (Celebrate Recovery news)
- Teach lesson from the *Celebrate Recovery Leader's Guide* or have a testimony
- Serenity Prayer
- No opportunity to share
- Mixed group
- Dismiss to open share groups or Newcomers 101
- Information table

cont.

Open Share Group

- Recovery issue specific
- Immediately follows large group meeting
- Gender specific
- One-hour meeting
- Share struggles and victories
- Acknowledge sobriety (chips)
- Open to newcomers
- Find a sponsor and/or an accountability partner
- Follow the five small group guidelines

Step Study Group

- Use *Celebrate Recovery* participant's guides
- Answer and discuss questions at the end of each lesson of the guides
- Follow the five small group guidelines
- Two-hour meeting
- Mixed recovery OR recovery issue specific
- High level of accountability
- Weekly attendance expected
- Gender specific

Newcomers 101

"Praise be to the God and Father of our Lord Jesus Christ, the Father of compassion and the God of all comfort, who comforts us in all our troubles, so that we can comfort those in any trouble with the comfort we ourselves receive from God." (2 Corinthians 1:3–4)

After the large group (8:00 to 9:00 p.m.) I suggest that you attend Newcomers 101. It is a group designed just for you. You only need to go to this group your first week. Why is it important? Because we have found that when someone comes to Celebrate Recovery for the first time he or she may be overwhelmed with feelings of fear, pain, humiliation, sadness, or hopelessness. The whole concept of recovery may be unfamiliar and a little frightening.

Selecting and identifying with an open share group may seem an impossible task.

Newcomers 101 will help you better understand what Celebrate Recovery at your local church is all about and you will be able to ask questions. The group will be divided into two parts: an informational large group meeting and an open share group. The following is a typical schedule:

1. Welcome and handing out of Solid Rock Coupons
The leaders of the group will welcome you and pass out Solid Rock Coupons, the coffee time hosted at the end of the meeting (or coupons for the meal the program provides before next week's meeting).

2. Opening prayer
After everyone is seated, a leader will open in prayer.

3. Showing the newcomers' video
The video will introduce you to leaders from different areas of recovery talking about the changes God and the program have made in their lives. Usually the senior pastor will share a few words about Celebrate Recovery and how it has changed their church.

4. The leaders will introduce themselves and briefly state the goal of the Newcomers 101
The goal of Newcomers 101 is to explain how Celebrate Recovery works and to help you find a group to attend next week. The newcomers group is a one-time attendance group only.

You will learn that the Newcomers' large group will be divided into a men's group and a women's group during the second half of the evening—just like the open share groups that are meeting throughout church.

Questions will be welcomed after the Newcomers' open share group sharing. However, questions are not a part of the regular open share groups.

5. Announcing time and place for Celebration Station and The Landing

These are programs for elementary school, junior high, and high school students. Celebrate Recovery is a place that the entire family can find healing in one program. (These programs may not yet be available at every Celebrate Recovery.)

6. Explaining the different components of the program

Very briefly the leaders will mention the tools of Celebrate Recovery: the *Celebrate Recovery Bible*, the four participant's guides, and the *Celebrate Recovery Journal. Life's Healing Choices* is the recommended book to better understand the eight recovery principles and to be encouraged by an additional sixteen great testimonies.

7. Reading the five small group guidelines

1. Keep your sharing focused on your own thoughts and feelings. Limit your sharing to three to five minutes.
2. There is no cross talk. Cross talk is when two individuals engage in conversation excluding all others. Each person is free to express their feelings without interruptions. (For the Newcomers 101 event, we break the cross talking guideline when we accept questions at the end of the sharing. At future meetings, this guideline will be obeyed. Otherwise, we will abide by the rest of the guidelines.)
3. We are here to support one another. We are not here to "fix one another."
4. Anonymity and confidentiality are basic requirements. What is shared in the group stays in the group. The only exception is when someone threatens to injure themselves or others.
5. Offensive language and graphic descriptions have no place in a Christ-centered recovery group.

8. Dividing into men's and women's small groups

You will be encouraged to give your first name, to state the group you can identify with, or just to say what brought you to Celebrate Recovery for the first time. Of course, you will have the opportunity to pass if you are not ready to share. If you decide to pass, you can meet with a leader one-on-one at the end of the meeting, while the rest of the group talks informally. Leaders will let everyone know that they are always available to answer any future questions.

9. Closing in prayer

The group will stand and a leader will pray the closing prayer.

Summary

Here's a quick review of the evening: The dinner or Bar-B-Que meets at 6:00 p.m., at 7:00 we meet for our large group time, and at 8:00 we break up into our smaller open share groups. After our groups, at 9:00, we go to Solid Rock Cafe for coffee and dessert. Remember, at the dinner and coffee, you can make new friends and start to form accountability partners and sponsors. You will learn more about building your accountability team in our large group meetings.

I know you will enjoy Celebrate Recovery! Just keep coming back! As I travel around the country, I hope to see you at a meeting.

Chapter 4

HOW CAN I GET MORE QUESTIONS ANSWERED ABOUT CELEBRATE RECOVERY?

The purpose of this chapter is to answer as many of your questions as possible. I want you to attend your first Celebrate Recovery meeting free of any doubts or fears and fully able to focus on God's power to help you remove your mask and start the recovery process.

So I asked Celebrate Recovery's leadership team to help me develop a list of Frequently Asked Questions to help you with any concerns.

Frequently Asked Questions (FAQs)

Q: What is Celebrate Recovery?
A: *The following is a list of things we ARE:*

- A safe place to share
- A refuge
- A place of belonging
- A place to care for others and be cared for
- Where respect is given to each member

- Where confidentiality is nonnegotiable
- A place to learn
- A place to grow and become strong again
- Where you can take off your mask
- A place for healthy challenges and healthy risks
- A possible turning point in your life

The following are the things we are NOT:

- A place for selfish control
- Therapy
- A place for secrets
- A place to look for dating relationships
- A place to rescue or be rescued by others
- A place for perfection
- A long-term commitment
- A place to judge others
- A quick fix

Q: How can I find a Celebrate Recovery near me?

A: Celebrate Recovery has a national website telling where groups meet all over the United States: *www.celebraterecovery.com*.

Q: Do I have to belong to the same denomination to go to Celebrate Recovery at the church where it is held?

A: No, everyone is welcome at Celebrate Recovery, no matter your denomination. You do not have to belong to a church to come to Celebrate Recovery.

Q: Do I have to be a Christian to attend?

A: No, all you have to do to qualify is to have a hurt, hang-up, or habit and a desire to get well.

Q: Is it okay for me to be in the same small group as a family member?

A: No, we feel that it is easier to be in a separate group so that you can feel safe to share more deeply. Sometimes we hold back when our family members are with us.

Q: Is it okay for me to take notes?

A: It is okay to take notes during the large group portion. We do, however, ask that during open share group you refrain from bringing out any note-taking materials, because it is distracting to others.

Q: Do I have to sign up to come to Celebrate Recovery?

A: No, just show up. You are welcome to arrive early if you would like to ask some questions before the group time starts. If not, we have a group that is offered for all first-time attendees. It tells a little about who we are and gives the participants a chance to ask questions.

Q: Are your leaders trained counselors or psychiatrists?

A: No. The group leaders are those who know what it is like to be lost, broken, or hurting. Your leaders have overcome the same issues that you are going through. They now are committed to helping you and others find hope and healing as well.

Q: How long will I need to attend Celebrate Recovery to find healing?

A: Healing from our hurts, hang-ups, and habits is a journey. If we surrender our lives to Christ, He saves us (Principle 3). The twelve steps and the eight principles help us work through the issues we face. For some, the journey lasts a year. For others, the journey can last a lifetime. The length of time depends on the depth of your hurts, hang-ups, and habits. Remember, that your hurts, hang-ups, and habits occurred over a long period of time. They will not go away overnight!

Q: I've heard people introduce themselves in a very different way at Celebrate Recovery than at most secular programs. Why is that?

A: In Celebrate Recovery, you will hear folks introduce themselves like this: *"My name is _____ and I am a grateful believer in Jesus Christ and I struggle with _____."* We do this in order to emphasize that though we do still struggle with hurts, hang-ups, and habits, our identity is in our relationship with Jesus Christ. He is the one and only true Higher Power.

Q: How do I know which group to go to?

A: Upon your first visit to Celebrate Recovery, it is highly recommended that you attend the ministry's Newcomer 101 group in order to get an overview of the program and an orientation to what groups are available.

Q: Do I have to buy the *Celebrate Recovery Bible* for the step study?

A: Although it is not required, it is highly recommended. The *Celebrate Recovery Bible* is a seamless tool for navigating the timeless recovery principles found in your step study and in Scripture. You will need a Bible.

Q: Why do I have to go to the large group? Can't we just go to an open share meeting and eliminate all of the singing and lessons and testimonies? What's the point of all that stuff?

A: The Celebrate Recovery large group time is structured to provide a starting place for the night. This time allows us to start the process of clearing our minds and preparing our hearts for the message or testimony that will be delivered that evening. It also gives us a time to connect with others before going into the small groups.

Q: What is the purpose for separate men's and women's groups? Why can't we have co-ed groups?

A: The purpose for Celebrate Recovery having gender-specific groups is that it provides another opportunity to have a safe place to share. Separate groups allow men to be open in their groups and speak freely about their issues, and the same for women. It also protects the groups from being a place for people who are looking to impress the opposite gender during their sharing by embellishing their story. And there are some people who are not comfortable talking in front of the opposite gender and will shut down and not share at all. It also eliminates a "dating" scene from developing within the groups.

Q: What is the difference between a sponsor and an accountability partner?

A: First of all, an accountability partner and sponsor should be the same gender as you. A sponsor is like a coach and an accountability partner is like a teammate. When you are out on the field and do something that goes the wrong way, your teammates are there to encourage you. When you return to the bench where your coach awaits, he/she is there to correct your methods and suggest a better way to try to prevent errors.

Q: How soon do I need to get a sponsor/accountability partner?

A: The sooner the better! The benefit of walking with a sponsor and/or accountability partner is that you will have support for every step along the road to recovery. The Bible tells us that we cannot do life alone, and therefore, we cannot do recovery alone. There will be times when temptation is overwhelming and you will need to contact someone to discuss the temptation and work out a solution to prevent a possible relapse.

Q: What do I do if my spouse or someone close to me relapses?

A: The great thing about Celebrate Recovery is that we are taught that we must first work on our own recovery. The hard thing to realize is that we are no good to anyone who is struggling if our recovery is not solid. We need to be supportive of our spouses and encourage them through their recovery, but we cannot fix them. Only as their relationship with God gets stronger will they be able to avoid relapse. When you come and learn all of the necessary tools of Celebrate Recovery, then you can be an example to your spouse that the program works. It can work for them too.

Q: Is Celebrate Recovery court-mandated approved?

A: We have found nationwide that many local courts recognize Celebrate Recovery as a proven and effective 12 Step program for alcohol- and drug-related mandates. However, we strongly suggest that you confirm with your local court to ensure that they approve Celebrate Recovery.

Q: Do you have any groups to help my teenage son or daughter?

A: Yes, we have a group called "The Landing." It is based on the same principles as Celebrate Recovery, but it presents them in a way that students will connect with. The lessons deliver hope-filled truths and real-life strategies for giving young people the tools for making wise choices and developing healthy patterns for living. The curriculum is experiential and includes small groups.

Q: Do you have groups for grade-school children?

A: Yes, we have a group called "Celebration Station." It is a pre-recovery program based on the same principles as Celebrate Recovery, but it presents them in a way that grade-school-aged children will understand. The age-appropriate lessons deliver hope-filled truths and real-life strategies for giving young children the tools on how to start making wise choices and developing healthy patterns for living. The curriculum is experiential and includes small groups.

Q: Are there Celebrate Recovery groups available in other countries? Is the curriculum available in other languages besides English?

A: Yes, there are groups in several countries around the world and they are making a big difference in people's lives. The curriculum is currently available in over twenty-four languages. For more information on either of these questions, you can check out *www.celebraterecoveryglobal.com*.

Q: I have a family member in another country—how can I get information on the groups available in each country?

A: You can find out more information about where groups are around the world by checking out *www.celebraterecovery global.com* or by emailing *bobwood@celebraterecoveryglobal .com*.

Q: Why are the Celebrate Recovery step studies so important and why do they take about a year to complete?

A: We learn about recovery and celebrate our victories in the large group. Then we share our struggles and victories in the open share groups. However, the "meat and potatoes" of recovery happens when we join a step study and answer the questions found in the four Celebrate Recovery participant's guides. Given the number of participants in a step study group, the process of moving through the guides can take from nine to twelve months of meeting weekly. The process of asking ourselves deep questions and finding healing does not happen overnight—but it does happen if we are willing to take this Christ-centered journey.

Q: What exactly does "codependency" mean?

A: Generally speaking, being "codependent" means that I value someone else's happiness and situation over my own. If I constantly make excuses for a loved one's behavior and not allow them to experience the consequences of their actions, I am operating in a state of "codependency." This term can sometimes be confused with "acting Christian," but in Celebrate Recovery we learn how to love others as Christ loves us and allow others to live their lives with their own choices. We learn what it means to have boundary lines that foster healthy relationships.

Q: Can I still go to my other secular recovery meeting if I attend Celebrate Recovery?

A: This is completely up to you. Attendance at Celebrate Recovery is a personal choice, just like attendance at any other program.

Q: Can I have a sponsor from a secular program?

A: Celebrate Recovery encourages participants to find their own sponsors, but we do have suggestions for things to consider before asking someone to fill this role. A sponsor should be the same gender, have at least one year of sobriety (preferably more), in the same area of recovery as you. A sponsor should also demonstrate a mature and growing relationship with Jesus Christ. With these characteristics, a good sponsor from a secular program will also honor the Celebrate Recovery process. Hopefully, they will attend Celebrate Recovery meetings with you as well.

Q: Why don't you have a group for _____?

A: Celebrate Recovery takes the role of leadership very seriously. Newcomers to recovery can be very vulnerable, and it is important that those leading the groups have walked through the process and found healing for themselves first. Therefore, the open share groups that are offered at an individual church will reflect the recovery journeys of the local leadership. All programs will offer a men's and women's group. The principles of recovery are the same for all issues, and participants can find support and help for their issue in any group. As the leadership of the program grows, more groups covering more specific recovery issues can be offered.

Q: I am not an addict. Why should I attend Celebrate Recovery?

A: Celebrate Recovery is for any kind of struggle in our lives. Less than a third of the people who attend Celebrate Recovery struggle with substance abuse—the rest may come for anger, marriage struggles, adult children on drugs, overeating, you name it! Many of us come because someone in our family is struggling. If a family member is struggling, it is affecting the whole family—and we need support too! Everybody needs recovery!

Q: What if I want to leave after the large group?

A: You are certainly welcome to do so—we will not hold you captive! However, it is important for you to know that this recovery process is much like baking a cake. If you leave one of the ingredients out of the recipe, it just won't taste the same. In the same way, in recovery there is a reason we have the three ongoing groups to the Celebrate Recovery process. We encourage everyone to jump in with both feet. Many people will say that they just don't have time to do all three components—the large group, the open share group, and the step study group. As a wise accountability partner once told me, "We need to spend as much time on our recovery as we have on our junk." Those who work the process by doing the proven three groups really see much more significant and longstanding growth. It truly does work if you work it and won't if you don't.

Q: I'm not a believer, but I have some issues I need to deal with. Can I still go to Celebrate Recovery?

A: Absolutely! We are a Christ-centered recovery ministry and are going to acknowledge God and His role in our recovery, but we do not require you to become a believer in order to attend and participate.

Q: How do I keep my attendance a secret from the rest of my family? I don't want them to know I have a problem.

A: Celebrate Recovery is a safe place to share your hurts, hang-ups, and habits because we follow five simple small group guidelines. They make the ministry safe. We honor confidentiality and anonymity. We don't tell others who attends Celebrate Recovery or who is in our groups. Everything that is shared in the groups stays there. Celebrate Recovery is a safe place to share our struggles.

CLOSING
THOUGHTS

As we come to the end of *Your First Step to Celebrate Recovery*, I want to congratulate you for preparing to begin this healing journey. As you choose what Celebrate Recovery group you will attend, and as you walk through the doors for the first time, I want you to know my prayers are with you! You will find others there who will walk alongside you on your road to recovery! This is only the beginning of what God has planned for you.

I would like to share one of my favorite prayers with you. It is called the Prayer for Serenity:

> *God, grant me the serenity*
> *to accept the things I cannot change,*
> *the courage to change the things I can,*
> *and the wisdom to know the difference.*
> *Living one day at a time,*
> *enjoying one moment at a time,*
> *accepting hardship as a pathway to peace,*
> *taking, as Jesus did, this sinful world as it is,*
> *not as I would have it;*
> *trusting that You will make all things right*
> *if I surrender to Your will;*
> *so that I may be reasonably happy in this life*
> *and supremely happy with You forever in the next. Amen.*
>
> Reinhold Niebuhr

In this prayer, we are asking God that we *be reasonably happy in this life*. That's what we have been really striving for as we work through the eight principles—a reasonable, healthy way to live life in the reality of today.

We are no longer expecting perfection in ourselves or others. As you work through Celebrate Recovery, it is my prayer that your definition of happiness will change. I hope you find that true happiness is in having a personal relationship with Jesus Christ. Happiness is being free from your hurts, hang-ups, and habits. Happiness is having honest and open relationships with others.

Just reading this book is not enough for your recovery. It's only the beginning. It takes commitment, and it takes relationships. That begins when you attend Celebrate Recovery for the first time and find people there to love and support you. If you already have a church family, start attending their Celebrate Recovery. If they do not have Celebrate Recovery yet, make an appointment with your pastor, share this book, and help start one!

I really want to know how you are doing. You can follow me on *www.Facebook.com/celebraterecovery*. I post almost daily. I'm also *@CRFounder* on Twitter. And please continue checking *www.celebraterecovery.com* for updates!

To God be the glory!
John Baker

Twelve Steps and Their Biblical Comparisons

1. We admitted we were powerless over our addictions and compulsive behaviors, that our lives had become unmanageable.

   "I know that nothing good lives in me, that is, in my sinful nature. For I have the desire to do what is good, but I cannot carry it out." (Romans 7:18)

2. We came to believe that a power greater than ourselves could restore us to sanity.

   "For it is God who works in you to will and to act according to his good purpose." (Philippians 2:13)

3. We made a decision to turn our lives and our wills over to the care of God.

   "Therefore, I urge you, brothers, in view of God's mercy, to offer your bodies as living sacrifices, holy and pleasing to God—this is your spiritual act of worship." (Romans 12:1)

4. We made a searching and fearless moral inventory of ourselves.

   "Let us examine our ways and test them, and let us return to the Lord." (Lamentations 3:40)

5. We admitted to God, to ourselves, and to another human being the exact nature of our wrongs.

   "Therefore confess your sins to each other and pray for each other so that you may be healed." (James 5:16)

6. We were entirely ready to have God remove all these defects of character.

   "Humble yourselves before the Lord, and he will lift you up." (James 4:10)

7. We humbly asked Him to remove all our shortcomings.

   "If we confess our sins, he is faithful and will forgive us our sins and purify us from all unrighteousness." (1 John 1:9)

8. We made a list of all persons we had harmed and became willing to make amends to them all.

   "Do to others as you would have them do to you." (Luke 6:31)

9. We made direct amends to such people whenever possible, except when to do so would injure them or others.

   "Therefore, if you are offering your gift at the altar and there remember that your brother has something against you, leave your gift there in front of the altar. First go and be reconciled to your brother; then come and offer your gift." (Matthew 5:23–24)

10. We continued to take personal inventory and when we were wrong, promptly admitted it.

    "So, if you think you are standing firm, be careful that you don't fall!" (1 Corinthians 10:12)

11. We sought through prayer and meditation to improve our conscious contact with God, praying only for knowledge of His will for us and power to carry that out.

    "Let the word of Christ dwell in you richly." (Colossians 3:16)

12. Having had a spiritual experience as the result of these steps, we try to carry this message to others and to practice these principles in all our affairs.

    "Brothers, if someone is caught in a sin, you who are spiritual should restore him gently. But watch yourself, or you also may be tempted." (Galatians 6:1)

How God Has Changed My Life through Celebrate Recovery

Allen R. — Celebrate Recovery is a mirror that allows me to see the things in my life that God wants to change.

Mary L. — Celebrate Recovery has taught me compassion, and with compassion came my healing.

Cory R. — Celebrate Recovery allowed me to finally see the woman of God I was designed to be!

Mark Z. — Before I was eating out of dumpsters. Now, with Celebrate Recovery, I'm living on God's Word.

Jeanne P. — Four years ago, I walked into my first Celebrate Recovery fellowship with fears and doubt. Through this blessed program, I have gained a stronger grasp on God's plan for my life.

Cheyenne S. — I started going to support my son but quickly found that God had much more planned! I've been in Celebrate

Recovery almost a year and have been healed with many, many blessings.

Wynette C. — I came to Celebrate Recovery a day after attempting suicide. I remember going up to get a blue chip, ready to surrender a life of drug abuse, depression, and suicide attempts. I stood before people whose eyes were focused on me, not with that usual judgmental stare but with a look of love and compassion. When I took that chip and sat down, it felt as though the weight of the world had been lifted off of my shoulders. At Celebrate Recovery I found love, acceptance, and sincere concern not only for my mental and physical well-being, but also for my spiritual well-being.

Yvette M. — Celebrate Recovery helps me with every aspect of my life!

Sherrie B. — Celebrate Recovery has helped me heal a lot of wounds that years of counseling could not heal. Because of Celebrate Recovery I have become a better mother and wife!

Sarah B. — I grew up in church and I've always known that God was the answer to my problems, but I was so bound by my hang-ups and struggles that I couldn't find peace. Celebrate Recovery is completely changing my life! For the first time I have hope and peace, while God is gradually shaping me into the woman He has called me to be.

Julie A. — I never felt "good enough for church," yet I wasn't "bad enough" for AA anymore. After twenty-five years in recovery, Celebrate Recovery brought what I was missing all along — the power of God to heal me.

Terie P. — Celebrate Recovery showed me that no matter how bad or how worthless I thought I was, God still loves me. I also learned that what people did to me was not my fault, but what I did to people I had to assume responsibility for. No matter how low on the ladder of life I feel, Jesus put me right up on the top rung by His sacrifice for me.

Michael B. — Five years ago I walked into a Celebrate Recovery program hating myself, hating others, and hating God. Today, through the healing and restoring grace of Jesus who I met at Celebrate Recovery, I'm in love with God, in love with the person who He has made me to be, and I'm the ministry leader of a beautiful Forever Family at the very same Celebrate Recovery program I walked into five years ago.

Janet R. — Celebrate Recovery helps me find a way out of the forest life gives me each day and gives me a special way to help hurting people heal!

Mary Beth F. — I worked my Celebrate Recovery steps in prison and when I was released I became a leader and a Sunday school teacher.

Jennifer E. — I first attended Celebrate Recovery to find out how to get and keep my husband sober. After working through a full step study, I realized I had just as much of a need to change. Six years later, he's sober (all through his journey in Celebrate Recovery) and I've worked more and more on own my issues. Today I am able to boast of my weakness and to help lead other women to find truth.

Andrew H. — When I first attended Celebrate Recovery, I didn't believe anything was wrong with me. After all, I had never messed with drugs or alcohol … what good was a 12-Step program for me? How wrong I was! Anger, lust, codependency … Celebrate Recovery is helping me allow God to put my life back in order. Thank you, John Baker, for allowing God to do His work through you!

Teresa L. — I had been a Christian for over thirty years, even in positions of leadership but never really experienced true freedom in Christ. After attending Celebrate Recovery and a step study, I was finally able to gain accountability, confess my sins to other godly women, and begin to see healing from codependency, divorce, abuse, and so much more, as things that had been hidden for so many years were finally brought into the light! It's more than a program; it's a way of life, and it works!

Mandi L. — I found Celebrate Recovery before I even knew who God was. Not only was Celebrate Recovery a turning point for my life, it was also a starting point for me to develop my relationship with God and to become a Christian.

Loretta D. — I came from secular recovery looking for a Christ-centered recovery program that could help me grow in my relationship with Christ, find support in maintaining my sobriety, and work on my very present issues of codependency. Celebrate Recovery was home for me!

Julie T. — My life has turned around because of Celebrate Recovery. I have made so many true friends who have encouraged me to do the hard things I had to do, with love and acceptance all the way.

James M. — Celebrate Recovery helps you learn to apply God's Word to the struggles in your own life, just as Jesus did in His temptation. There is power in the Word and Celebrate Recovery teaches you how to apply it.

Malinda C. — Celebrate Recovery helped me see that it doesn't matter where we came from. What matters is where we are going.

Melodie W. — God changed my life through Celebrate Recovery by giving me sisters who understand because they have been where I have been. Trust and safety, there's no feeling like it in the world. When we're together at meetings, I feel Jesus' arms around us!

Marvin M. — Through Celebrate Recovery, God took a messed-up pastor and gave him a second chance.

Darlene M. — Celebrate Recovery was the open hand I needed to lift me out of the hell of my addiction and into true relationship with God.

Elmer D. — Celebrate Recovery is God with "skin on" for the things we all face today.

Wendy F. — I came to Celebrate Recovery broken and needing healing from abuse in my childhood. Years of counseling touched the surface, but didn't do the deep work that is happening now through a step study. I stay with Celebrate Recovery because it helps me find hope for each day.

Marty K. — I finally realized I mattered to God!

John M. — Thanks to some great people at Celebrate Recovery, I am finally at peace with God and myself. It is an awesome feeling. Today, I have a smile that nothing can take away and I mean — nothing!

Fran H. — Celebrate Recovery works if you work it — and you are worth it!

Diane C. — For eighteen years I kept God in my bookcase on a shelf. I never allowed Him to heal what He so desperately wanted to until I walked through the doors of Celebrate Recovery! Since that day, over five years ago, I have grown in Christ and am loving life as never before! Thank you, God and Pastor John.

Debbie H. — Celebrate Recovery took a very depressed, lonely woman and made her whole again! Me! It was nice to know there were several depressed ladies in my group and by working through the eight principles, we all found victory in Christ. You can find it as well! Praise God!

Jonathan S. — In Celebrate Recovery, I found the power in Jesus Christ to stop doing the things that caused me and my family so much pain.

Marianne S. — Codependency was my life. I hit rock bottom when I found out my husband was having an affair and addicted to porn. Shortly after, we started attending a Celebrate Recovery at our church and my life began to change. Celebrate Recovery gave me tools, strength, family, comfort, and a place where I could feel safe to be myself. I asked that my husband attend with me if he wanted our marriage to work. Celebrate Recovery saved our marriage! We are now ministry leaders and my husband is now a state rep for Celebrate Recovery! This program works and saves lives through God's amazing grace!

Karen R. — Through Celebrate Recovery I found help, healing, and a deeper, restored relationship with God. I've learned boundaries, communication skills, and how to have healthy relationships. I've learned how to trust God and others again. I've learned how to focus on the truth and not the trials. Thank You, God, for Celebrate Recovery.

Sue V. — Before Celebrate Recovery, I was a miserable mess. I was alone and I was an out-of-control glutton. But when I turned my mess completely over to God, He took it, made me new, and turned my mess into a message. Today, I have a life in Christ and a testimony that glorifies God. And rather than an abundance of food, I'm now enjoying an abundant life filled with the fruit of the Spirit. And this fruit—love, joy, peace, and self-control—is far better than any food I ever binged on!

Harry H. — I lived fifty-five years believing that God existed, but was unable to feel a true relationship with Jesus Christ. Through Celebrate Recovery and witnessing the never-ending victories in others' lives, I learned that I AM a son of the King — that He had always been with me and always will be. All I had to do was surrender, and His light warmed my soul and showed me the way to live in Him!

Janet C. — I came to Celebrate Recovery wearing a mask that said, "I'm fine; how can I help you?" Now, four and a half years later, the mask is gone, and I've been healed from past events I thought I'd gotten over. I know I have worth because God loves me just the way I am.

Tim M. — After being stuck in an addiction to pornography for twenty-five years, Celebrate Recovery offered me something that nothing else had … HOPE!

Micah H. — Through Celebrate Recovery I have found Christ-centered accountability — men of God who support me, confront me, cry with me, and celebrate with me. It is truly "iron sharpening iron" so that we can bring glory to God.

Brenda Y. — God has brought me to my knees through the struggles of my marriage, my codependency, and my husband's sexual addictions. I was ready to run away from the problem and let the wind carry me away. Celebrate Recovery provided a solid foundation to hold on to through my time of need. Praise God for bringing me to my knees; my pride was strong and I was not easily bent. God knows what is best even when I can't see it.

Lynne F. — The hardest part about coming to Celebrate Recovery the first time was getting across the parking lot from my car to the door. But I was welcomed with genuine smiles and love, not pity. The easiest part of coming to Celebrate Recovery is making the decision to keep coming back!

Amber A. — Because of past hurts, I took a detour off the path that God had intended for me. I got lost, hit a few bumps, and got a few cuts and scrapes. Because of God and through Celebrate Recovery, I am no longer lost. My feet are firmly planted back on His path and this time the bumps aren't so bad and the cuts and scrapes don't hurt as much. Thank you, Jesus, and thank you, Celebrate Recovery!

Jeff P. — I found my sobriety in secular recovery, but I kept my sobriety by starting a Celebrate Recovery at my church. Celebrate Recovery showed me what the Bible had to say about recovery and allowed my church to see the healing benefits of a support group ministry.

Ingrid B. — Celebrate Recovery has taught me what true mercy and grace is all about. Though I have been and worked in church most of my life, Celebrate Recovery has shown me what God's true love looks like. It is now my first ministry.

Mary S. — Even though I was full of anxiety walking into Celebrate Recovery that very first time, I was even more anxious that the rest of my life would be the continuing cycle of disappointments, failures, and pain I had experienced so far. Celebrate Recovery has changed my life into one full of joy, hope, peace, and just sheer happiness. To get something I never had, I had to do something I never did — go to Celebrate Recovery!

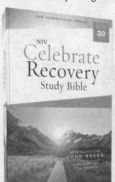

Celebrate Recovery®

LEADER'S GUIDE

There is a way the church can help the wounded move beyond their hurts, habits, and hang-ups to experience the forgiveness of Christ. Celebrate Recovery® helps the church fulfill its role as Christ's healing agent. You don't have to lead alone. To lead people forward in spiritual, physical, and emotional restoration is to walk in the footsteps of Christ. And that's why the *Celebrate Recovery Leader's Guide* is so important.

With everything you need to encourage lasting life-change, the leader's guide is the best way to facilitate Celebrate Recovery in your church and help people look forward to a whole new future.

9780310131540

The *Celebrate Recovery Leader's Guide* includes:
- Fresh testimonies
- A 90-day start-up strategy
- A clear, easy-to-follow format
- Step-by-step instructions for each meeting
- Guide for conducting leader training
- Teaching notes for the 25 lessons of *The Journey Begins* (Participant Guides 1-4)
- Overview of the 25 lessons of *The Journey Continues* (Participant Guides 5-8)

Along with a willing heart, this leader's guide is invaluable for leading men and women forward in complete restoration and transformation through Christ.

ater critic for a Dublin newspaper, the *Evening Mail*. A couple of Bram's stories were published, but they didn't earn him much money or attention. It was his volunteer newspaper work that led to a big change in Bram's life.

Back when Bram had been in college, he had seen a play starring an actor named Henry Irving. Bram thought Irving was the greatest actor in the world. Almost ten years later, Irving was appearing in Dublin, playing the lead role in *Hamlet*. Bram wrote a very complimentary review. In gratitude, Irving sent Bram a backstage pass for the next performance. The two men met and became friends. Their friendship became the most important thing in the world to Bram. As you'll see, it's difficult to say whether that was a good thing or not.

In 1878, two years after they met, Henry Irving offered Bram Stoker the job of managing a theater in London. The job was a very demanding one. Stoker had to manage the theater's 120 employees, keep track of the theater's money, and arrange the actors' international tours. He also served as a kind of personal secretary to Irving, who was by then one of the most famous actors in the world. However, Stoker didn't hesitate for a moment. He quit his government job, married his beautiful 19-year-old fiancée, Florence Balcombe, and moved to London. Within a year, he and Florence had a son, whom they named Irving Noel Stoker.

Henry Irving was a man with a tremendously strong, even overwhelming, personality. He seemed to have an almost hypnotic effect on Bram, who was quiet and mild-mannered. Bram was so devoted to his friend and employer that he often seemed more concerned about Irving's welfare than that of his own family. When the actor traveled, Bram went with him, making sure that Irving had everything that he needed. As time went on, Florence grew to resent her husband's involvement with Irving. Florence and Bram never divorced, but their relationship grew very chilly. Feeling the same kind of resentment, their son eventually dropped "Irving" as his first name and was known just as "Noel."

While all this was going on, Bram continued to write stories in his free time. In 1890, he told friends he was thinking of writing a novel about a vampire Count, whom he planned to name Wampyr. But that summer, while spending some time in the English seaside town of Whitby, he checked a history book out of the public library. In it he read about a 15th century Romanian prince known as Vlad the Impaler. (He was called "the

Impaler" for his habit of cutting off his enemies' heads and impaling them on spikes.) Vlad sometimes called himself "Dracula," which is based on the Romanian word for either "dragon" or "devil." Bram instantly changed his plan and borrowed Vlad the Impaler's devilish name for his Count. And, of course, he also borrowed the town of Whitby—especially its cemetery—as the setting for Lucy and Mina's first encounters with the vampire.

Dracula was published in 1897. It did not create much excitement at the time. Bram continued working for the theater until Irving's death in 1906. (Bram was so upset by the actor's death that he himself had a mild stroke.) Bram then retired from the theater and continued to write fiction and newspaper articles until his own death in 1912. He never had any idea what a success his novel would become. It wasn't until 1931, when Universal Studios made the movie version of *Dracula,* starring Bela Lugosi, that the novel really caught on. It has never been out of print since and has been translated into dozens of languages. Bram's widow, Florence, lived until 1937, so she did earn some money from her husband's now-famous novel.

Bram wrote dozens of short stories and

several more novels (the best known are *The Jewel of Seven Stars,* published in 1903, and *The Lair of the White Worm,* 1911). Most people agree, though, that *Dracula* is by far Bram's best work. It seems to be the work that he poured his heart and soul into, and readers have responded to its wonderful qualities for more than a century.

The greatest mystery of Bram Stoker's life seems to be this: How did this quiet, mild-mannered man—some even say a boring man—produce *Dracula,* one of the most horrifying books ever written? Bram spent his own adult life taking care of a bossy actor with an extremely strong personality. It seems as though Bram had almost no personality of his own. It doesn't make sense that Bram could create a character like Dracula!

Or does it?

Bram isn't talking, but is it possible that he borrowed themes from his own life as he wrote *Dracula?* Could the powerful, evil, but somehow strangely attractive Count be inspired by . . . Henry Irving? Could poor Renfield in his cell, irresistably drawn to the Count and longing to be powerful like him, be a little like . . . Bram Stoker? Could the whole novel be seen as a sort of revenge against the man to whom Bram devoted his own life?

We'll never know. Bram never said a word against his former employer; he even published a book called *Personal Reminiscences of Henry Irving* in 1906. There's no way of knowing if Bram ever regretted his decision to live in the shadow of the famous actor.

But life has a way of evening things out. Today, few people remember the name of Henry Irving. Mention the name of Bram Stoker, on the other hand, and you'll likely hear, "Oh, yeah; he wrote *Dracula*, didn't he? Man, I bet he was one amazing guy."

ABOUT THIS EDITION

In preparing this edition of *Dracula*, we asked ourselves two questions.

The first is this: Why do today's readers still like *Dracula*, a book that is more than one hundred years old?

The second: What could keep today's readers from enjoying *Dracula* as much as earlier readers have?

The answer to the first question was clear. *Dracula* is a terrific story which features an unforgettable central character. Our fascination with vampires has not lessened one bit since Stoker's day, as shown by the steady production of vampire movies, novels by Anne Rice and other modern authors, and the popular TV series *Buffy the Vampire Slayer*. The frightening, intriguing Count Dracula is the foundation for all these later creations. Modern readers are every bit as interested in his story as their grandparents were.

In answer to the second question, we found a number of elements that could interfere with a modern reader's appreciation for *Dracula*. For one thing, Stoker expected his novel to be read by 19th-century Europeans, not 21st-century Americans. He makes many references to European culture, history, geography, and daily life that would be unfamiliar and confusing to many modern readers. Another possible "stumbling block" was Stoker's decision to include long passages of dialogue by minor characters who spoke in a non-standard kind of "working man's English." These passages would have amused and interested Stoker's original audience, but they are hard to understand today. One more obstacle to today's reader was the attention Stoker gave to inventions that were new in his time, including shorthand dictation, the typewriter, and the phonographic dictation machine. Stoker was using these technologies to make a contrast between the ways of the ancient Count and the modern world. Today's readers, however, would probably not understand Stoker's point.

In order to make *Dracula* the most enjoyable experience possible for today's readers, we have revised or eliminated material that fell into these categories, as well as several others. We have done so hoping that Bram Stoker himself would enjoy the prospect of his masterpiece being appreciated by a new century of readers.

ABOUT THE BOOK

In *Dracula*, Bram Stoker introduced the term *Undead*. He was referring to the Count, but the term could be applied to his novel as well. It's a book that is as alive today as it ever was.

Since it was first published in 1897, *Dracula* has been re-issued in more than three hundred editions and nearly fifty languages. The Count is probably the most filmed character in history: at least eight movie versions have been made of Stoker's novel, and many, many more films have been inspired by it. (A very short list of such movies includes such titles as *Dracula's Daughter*, *Duckula*,

Blacula, Shadow of the Vampire, Blade, Dracula: Dead and Loving It, and *Love at First Bite.*) At academic conferences, professors trade scholarly papers about *Dracula.* Travel agencies offer Dracula tours of Transylvania and cemetery walks in Whitby. There are operas, ballets, musicals, prequels, sequels, TV shows, cartoons, and plays that owe their existence to Stoker's creation. (And let's not forget *Sesame Street*'s "The Count" or Count Chocula chocolate-flavored cereal!)

Has any other work of fiction had that much effect on popular culture? It's hard to think of one. Sure, there are other well-known horror characters such as Frankenstein (also created in a classic novel), the Mummy, and the Wolfman. But their fame today is limited mostly to Halloween costumes. None of them receives the very serious attention that is given to Count Dracula.

What is it about *Dracula* that has fascinated so many people for so many years? The answer to that question has several parts.

First, there is the central theme: vampirism. Bram Stoker didn't invent the idea of the vampire. As Professor Van Helsing says in the novel, "the vampire is known everywhere that men have ever lived. In old Greece, in old Rome, in Germany, France, India, China, there he is, and has always been." Throughout history, people have been fascinated by the idea of men and women who cannot die, but who feed off the blood of the living. From time to time in ancient Europe, waves of "vampire hysteria" caused people to be arrested and even executed as vampires.

Where did this belief in vampires come from? Probably blood-sucking creatures such as vampire bats (yes, they really exist) and spiders first put the idea into people's minds. And while there are no genuine immortal vampires such as Count Dracula, there have been cases of mentally ill individuals who had an unnatural desire to drink human blood. At its core, though, the belief in vampires has grown out of the universal fear of death. Immortality—living forever—is an idea that has both fascinated and repelled people from the dawn of time. They've wondered, "What would it take to live forever?" One possible answer is what Renfield tells Dr. Seward: "The blood is the life."

The search for immortality is related to another major reason why *Dracula* has enjoyed so much popularity for so long. People are naturally attracted to subjects that are taboo—in other words, forbidden. Living forever is a taboo subject, because a person who refuses to die is seen as defying the laws of God and nature. Other taboo subjects are hinted at in the book. For instance, Lucy, and later Mina, are strangely, almost romantically drawn to the Count, even though they know him to be very evil. Mina warns Jonathan that she finds the Count irresistible, and that she will lie to him, her beloved husband, in order to go to the vampire. Jonathan Harker wants the beautiful vampire women to kiss him, and later, Professor Van Helsing is so attracted to these women that he imagines himself allowing them to make him a vampire, too. Part of the thrill of reading *Dracula* comes from watching the characters struggle with these forbidden desires.

The characters in *Dracula*, too, help make the story attractive. Chief among them, of course, is the Count himself. It was a stroke of genius for Stoker to make Count Dracula what he is: a rich, well-educated nobleman who can be charming when he chooses. As he prepared to write *Dracula*, Stoker read all the old vampire myths and legends that he could find. Most described vampires as ugly, repulsive monsters. Stoker realized he wanted to create quite a different kind of vampire. By combining the old beliefs with his own touches, the author invented a character that is both terrifying and fascinating. The Count is all the more horrifying because of his good manners and charm.

Poor doomed Lucy is a lovely, flirtatious young woman who wonders why she can't marry three men at once, rather than make any of them unhappy. Her best friend Mina is a little more level-headed, and therefore better equipped to help defeat the Count. Jonathan Harker represents a very modern sort of man. He is highly intelligent, but he is so logical and businesslike that he seems very nearly stupid at times. Especially in the first several chapters, while he is living in Dracula's castle, he simply can't accept what he is seeing. After the terrifying scene in which he realizes the Count has no reflection, and Dracula then lunges at his throat, the thing Jonathan seems most upset about is that he has lost his shaving mirror!

Professor Van Helsing, on the other hand, is a man who understands the old, magical world that is home to Dracula. It is his job to convince the young people around him that the world is full of things that cannot be fully explained—such as vampires. At the same time, he is a modern scientist, and this is a great advantage. For Dracula is not a modern man. When he finds the letter Jonathan has written to Mina in shorthand, he is enraged because he cannot read it. (Shorthand was a new invention in Stoker's day, and the author used it to represent modern technology.) Van Helsing, therefore, is the perfect vampire-hunter, combining the ways of the old world with the discoveries of the new.

But above all, *Dracula* succeeds because it's a great story. It has romance and horror, great evil and selfless good, friendship and courage, loss and triumph. And over all, it has the presence of the Count: rarely seen, always felt, and endlessly terrifying. He is a character too fascinating to confine to Bram Stoker's book, and so we have seen his image in a countless number of movies, TV shows, and other popular media. Jonathan Harker may have cut off Dracula's head, but as generations of readers know, Dracula never really died.